VINCENZO VENEZIA

love **bombing**

Love or Manipulation? How to Recognize Emotional Traps, Break Free from Manipulators, and Rediscover Your Inner Strength

© **Copyright 2024 by Vincenzo Venezia - All rights reserved.**

The content contained within this book may not be reproduced, duplicated or transmitted without direct written permission from the author or the publisher.

Under no circumstances will any blame or legal responsibility be held against the publisher, or author, for any damages, reparation, or monetary loss due to the information contained within this book; either directly or indirectly.

Legal Notice:

This book is copyright protected. This book is only for personal use. You cannot amend, distribute, sell, use, quote or paraphrase any part, or the content within this book, without the consent of the author or publisher.

Disclaimer Notice:

Please note the information contained within this document is for educational and entertainment purposes only. All effort has been executed to present accurate, up-to-date, and reliable, complete information. No warranties of any kind are declared or implied. Readers acknowledge that the author is not engaging in the rendering of legal, financial, medical or professional advice.

ASIN: 979-12-81498-71-6

Contents

Introduction	1
Chapter 1: What is Love Bombing?	7
Chapter 2: The Stages of Love Bombing	22
Chapter 3: Who Is the Love Bomber?	45
Chapter 4: The Effects of Love Bombing on the Victim	73
Chapter 5: What to Do If You Are a Victim of Love Bombing	90
Chapter 6: When to Decide Whether to Stay or Leave	107
Chapter 7: Building Healthy and Authentic Relationships	123
Conclusion	139

Introduction

"Love bombing." A term that sounds both romantic and dangerous at the same time. It might evoke images of overwhelming gestures of love, passionate declarations, of a flame burning brightly. However, beneath the dazzling surface of this expression lies one of the most insidious and subtle forms of emotional manipulation.

Anyone who has ever experienced a whirlwind romance knows how thrilling it can be. A new love that sweeps you off your feet, pulling you into a whirlwind of attention, affection, and promises. Everything feels perfect—those small, tender gestures make your heart race, and the promises of a future together fuel dreams and hopes. But what happens when that intensity, which initially felt so captivating, starts to become overwhelming? When those affectionate gestures and sweet words begin to feel too good to be true? And most importantly, what happens when you discover that this much-lauded love is nothing more than a strategy of control?

Love bombing is a phenomenon that typically occurs at the start of a relationship, where one partner overwhelms the other with affection and attention to such a degree that it leaves them disoriented. The relationship seems like something out of a fairytale: constant messages, unexpected gifts, promises of a perfect and unique future together. At first, these gestures might seem like the expressions of genuine, passionate love. However, this strategy, often used by people with narcissistic traits or emotional manipulation tendencies, aims to create a deep bond in a very short time, only to use it later as a weapon of control and domination.

But love bombing doesn't just manifest in words. Alongside seemingly sweet phrases like *"You mean everything to me, I can't live without you"* or *"No one will ever love you like I do,"* there are affectionate gestures that appear genuine but conceal much darker intentions. Incessant messages, extravagant gifts, and constant surprises may look like signs of deep love, but when they become suffocating, they turn into clear indicators of emotional control. What initially seems like a demonstration of dedication, over time reveals its true nature.

Some of the declarations that accompany love bombing are laden with emotional pressure. Statements like *"I don't understand how you lived without me"* or *"You have to trust me, I know what's best for us"* may seem caring and protective, but in reality, they are paired with actions that consolidate a kind of emotional dominance over the other. Persistent invitations to spend all your time together, possessive attitudes disguised as concern, or disproportionate attention are often used as tools to limit the other partner's freedom. Even everyday expressions like *"Why don't you spend more time with me?"* or *"I'm doing this for your own good"* can become part of a manipulative behavior, where every caring gesture hides an underlying desire for control.

These declarations, seemingly harmless or even romantic, often accompanied by affectionate gestures like expensive gifts or small surprises, are actually means to trap the other person in a web of emotional obligations. When a partner constantly uses phrases like *"You're my only reason to live"* or *"I don't know what I'd do if you left me,"* and pairs them with relentless attention, the line between genuine love and manipulation becomes increasingly blurred. Love, once a mutual nourishment, transforms into a kind of emotional prison where the other partner feels suffocated but unable to break free.

Behind these gestures and words, which appear full of passion and devotion, lies a dangerous game where love becomes a tool for gaining power over the other. The generous gifts, constant displays of affection, and promises of a perfect life together are often masks that hide a deeper need for control. The goal is no longer to build a healthy, equal relationship, but to bind the other partner, making them dependent and submissive.

Love bombing is insidious precisely for this reason: it starts with an irresistible seduction, made of words and gestures anyone would want to receive in a relationship, but over time it reveals itself as a trap. The boundaries between love and manipulation become increasingly blurred until they disappear altogether. The victimized partner finds themselves trapped in a dynamic where control is exercised under the guise of love.

Popular culture doesn't help distinguish these dynamics. Movies, TV shows, and romantic songs often glorify the idea of all-consuming love, of a passion that justifies every behavior, even toxic ones. Think of the idealized love stories we're told: extreme gestures of jealousy, possessiveness, and devotion are often mistaken for demonstrations of true love. The expression "I can't live without you," so celebrated in many romantic tales, is often seen as a love promise rather than a warning sign. This kind of narrative idealizes relationships marked by intensity and drama, obscuring the signs of manipulation and control that might be lurking behind these behaviors.

However, not everyone falls victim to love bombing so easily. Certain personalities are more inclined to use it: the narcissist, who needs constant validation of their worth; the manipulator, who always wants to feel in control; or the seducer, who views every new relationship as another conquest to add to their tally. Likewise, some people are more vulnerable to this form of manipulation: those who are desperately seeking approval, those just coming out of a painful relationship, or those who tend to prioritize others' needs over their own.

We will analyze who the love bombers are and who is at risk of becoming their victim to better understand the dynamics fueling this phenomenon and how we can protect ourselves.

Throughout this book, we will explore love bombing in all its nuances: from its origin as a psychological phenomenon to its representation in pop culture, from scientific studies explaining its dynamics to tools for recognizing and defending against it. We will learn to distinguish genuine love from constructed love, to recognize warning signs, and to understand that love should never make us feel trapped or suffocated.

Because true love is made of freedom, respect, and balance. And the difference between a sincere gesture and a manipulative one can make all the difference between a relationship that enriches us and one that destroys us.

But this book isn't just for those who have been hurt, for those who have lived the nightmare behind the mask of romance. It's for anyone who wants to protect themselves, for those who wish to experience love with awareness and without fear. It's not about being suspicious of every affectionate gesture but about learning to recognize the moment when love stops nourishing us and starts consuming us. This book is for those who believe it's worth learning to recognize true love, in all its most beautiful forms, and to steer clear of that which only bears love's name.

Because, in the end, we all deserve to be truly loved—without games, without masks, without manipulation. And every step toward this awareness is a step toward a freer and happier life.

Chapter 1: What is Love Bombing?

Origin of the Term and Historical Context

The term "love bombing" might seem like a recent creation, perhaps one of those expressions born in the contemporary language of social media, where relationships are often reduced to hashtags and memes. But its origin is older and far less innocent than one might think.

The term first appeared in the 1970s when it was used to describe a technique adopted by certain religious cults to recruit new members. "Love bombing" was a literal bombardment of love, affection, and attention, a reception so warm and overwhelming that it made anyone feel like the most special and loved individual in the world. As soon as a potential recruit approached the community, they were surrounded by smiles, hugs, kind words, and promises of a glorious future where they would always be accepted, understood, and valued. The goal? To create an emotional dependency, a bond so strong that the thought of leaving became difficult, if not impossible.

Cults quickly realized that human beings are starved for love, especially those who feel lonely, confused, or searching for a sense of belonging. For these individuals, love, or the appearance of it, can become a beacon in the midst of a storm. In a world that often feels cold and indifferent, the idea of being welcomed into a warm, unconditional embrace, of finally feeling "seen" and accepted for who you are, is an irresistible temptation. The thirst for connection is universal; in some way, we are all victims of it. But for those desperately seeking a safe place where they feel important, that "bombardment of love" can seem like an answer to their most intimate prayers.

And this is why love bombing becomes such a powerful weapon in the hands of those who seek control: it offers a promise of absolute love and emotional security, a refuge from the uncertainties of the outside world. Imagine being greeted with smiles, comforting words, and constant flattery. *"You're special," "You belong with us," "You're finally home."* It's an injection of security that acts as a balm on the wounds of loneliness and insecurity.

But, as often happens, that initial love is just the bait. Once the person feels safe within the group, when they begin to believe that they have finally found their place, the dynamic changes. Slowly, almost imperceptibly, the unconditional love becomes conditional: *"We love you, but..."* And that "but" translates into increasingly demanding requests. It starts with small things: *"Could you come to more meetings?"*, "You should donate something to support the community." Then, the demands grow: more time, more money, more dedication. Now love seems to come with a price.

The love that once seemed generous and selfless turns into a bond. The demands become pressing: *"If you really love us, you'll do this for us,"* *"Your commitment is proof of your love."* And so, what began as sweet seduction evolves into a form of emotional coercion. The underlying message is clear: your value and belonging depend on your compliance.

This dynamic is particularly powerful because it exploits one of the deepest human needs: the need to be accepted. Under the pressure of the group, saying "no" becomes difficult, distinguishing between love and control, between belonging and captivity, becomes challenging. Any attempt at rebellion is seen as betrayal, a sign of ingratitude toward those who offered "so much love." And thus, the individual finds themselves trapped in an invisible web of expectations, where love, which was supposed to be liberating, becomes a new form of slavery.

Over the years, the term "love bombing" has begun to transcend the boundaries of religious communities, finding fertile ground in the context of romantic relationships. It was adopted by psychologists and therapists to describe the behavior of individuals who, in the early stages of a relationship, overwhelm their partner with affection and attention in a nearly suffocating manner. This phenomenon, which begins with a storm of sweet words, gifts, and grand gestures, follows a precise trajectory: building a bond quickly, establishing emotional dependency, and, ultimately, assuming control.

In recent years, with the growing awareness of narcissistic behaviors and toxic dynamics in relationships, the term "love bombing" has entered common language. It has become a way to describe a type of emotional manipulation that exploits the deepest human needs: to be loved, to feel important, to belong to something special.

However, as the term's popularity grew, its understanding became blurred. In a world where true love and toxic love are often confused, the concept of "love bombing" reminds us that not everything that glitters is gold. It's a reminder that love, as desirable and powerful as it is, can also be used as a tool of power and control.

Love in Popular Culture: Between Myths and Manipulation

Popular culture plays a significant role in shaping our perception of love. Movies, TV shows, songs, and books often present an ideal of love that is passionate, overwhelming, and sometimes even suffocating. This type of representation affects not only how we perceive our relationships but also how we react to situations that may seem romantic on the surface but hide dangerous dynamics, like love bombing.

A recurring example is the myth of "love at first sight." How many times have we seen in movies that scene where two people meet and, within moments, fall madly in love? Immediately after, everything becomes a race to declare eternal love, overcoming incredible obstacles and proving that passion is the true glue of a relationship. This type of narrative leads us to believe that love must be immediate, visceral, and all-encompassing, pushing us to idealize relationships that burn quickly and intensely.

However, in many of these romantic tales, there is a lack of balanced representation of mutual respect, the gradual development of trust, and the need for personal space. Instead, obsessive love is often glorified, where one partner cannot live without the other, where jealousy is seen as proof of devotion, and intimacy is accelerated at the expense of individual freedom. This representation becomes dangerous because it normalizes behaviors that, in real life, can be the first signs of emotional manipulation.

Love bombing exploits these romantic myths. Individuals who engage in it know that many people long for an intense love story, like the ones portrayed in the media. Consequently, they replicate these models with grand gestures and flashy declarations, fueling the illusion of having found perfect love. Think of phrases like *"I can't live without you"* or *"We're meant to be together,"* which in popular narratives are presented as sincere declarations of deep love, but in a toxic relationship, can be used to create emotional dependency.

In many romantic comedies or love dramas, possessive or obsessive behavior is mistaken for authentic love. Characters who send constant messages, give disproportionate gifts, or follow their beloved everywhere are portrayed as individuals who "do anything" for their love. The narrative teaches us that true love requires sacrifice, exaggerated gestures, and absolute dedication, even at the cost of one's identity and freedom. These gestures, in fiction, always lead to a happy ending, reinforcing the false belief that the more intense and overwhelming a relationship is, the more genuine it is.

The problem is that real life doesn't work that way. In reality, these displays of love are nothing more than red flags. When someone speeds up the pace of a relationship too quickly, invading every aspect of your life with declarations and gestures that are too intense, too soon, it might not be love, but a form of control in disguise. Love bombing feeds off these myths and uses them to manipulate those who are seeking a romantic relationship similar to the ones portrayed in films and songs.

Another aspect of popular culture that favors love bombing is the idea that true love must be difficult. In many stories, we see couples who go through dramatic moments, separations and reconciliations, misunderstandings and jealousies, but in the end, they find a way to be together. This myth of tormented love makes us believe that difficulties are a natural and necessary part of every relationship. So, when a partner puts pressure on us, or makes us feel guilty for not immediately reciprocating the same intensity of feelings, we might be led to think that we are simply experiencing the normal challenges of a great love story.

This belief makes it even harder to recognize love bombing. Those who practice it can easily justify their actions with the idea that "true love requires effort" or "I'm just trying to show how much I care about you." The victim may confuse signs of manipulation with the normal difficulties of a relationship, believing that if they endure long enough, everything will work out, just like in the movies.

Recognizing the Myths and Finding the Truth

Recognizing the influence of popular culture on our expectations of love is the first step to defending ourselves from love bombing. Understanding that true love does not need to be tumultuous or characterized by grand gestures helps us distinguish between a partner who genuinely loves us and one who seeks to manipulate us. Healthy love does not need exaggerated demonstrations, does not make us feel indebted, and, above all, does not suffocate us.

There are love stories in real life that are not told by the media: relationships where mutual respect and personal growth are at the center, where gestures of affection are sincere and without ulterior motives. These are relationships where love blooms slowly, where there is space to be yourself without fear of being judged or controlled. They are relationships that do not need spectacle to be deep and fulfilling.

In the end, love should never be a battle or a theatrical performance. It doesn't need to make itself known with fireworks. True love is often quiet, patient, and grows over time. And most importantly, it never needs to manipulate or control to exist.

The Difference Between Authentic Love and Manipulation

Authentic love and love bombing may look similar on the surface. Both can start with grand gestures of affection, sweet words, and promises of a future together. However, there is a fundamental difference that separates these two realities: **intention and mutual respect**.

Authentic love is built slowly, like a garden that requires time to grow. It doesn't need to force emotions or rush things. In a healthy relationship, every gesture, every word, is a gift free from hidden conditions. There is no rush to possess the other, no anxiety to control them. Genuine love is based on a balance of giving and receiving, where both people feel safe being themselves, without fear of being judged or manipulated.

In love bombing, however, the urgency is palpable. There is a rush that pushes everything to the maximum from the very beginning. This type of behavior often includes grand gestures, flashy declarations, unrealistic promises of the future, as if every moment needs to be a romantic drama. *"I can't live without you," "You're the love of my life, I knew it from the moment I saw you," "Let's make plans for our future right away."* These are phrases that can make your head spin, but too often hide an intent of possession.

The essential difference lies in **freedom and respect**. Authentic love leaves space, allows you to breathe. It gives you time to express your needs and fears. It invites you to grow together with the other person but does not try to force this growth according to a hidden agenda. It doesn't need to reduce the other to property, to something to control or mold. On the contrary, it is based on accepting the other for who they are, flaws and all, and on a mutual desire to build something together, one step at a time.

Love bombing, on the other hand, often seeks to bind the other person quickly, creating a dependency dynamic. The gestures are amplified, exaggerated, and always too much, too soon. There's a rush to accelerate intimacy, to speed through emotional milestones to create a quick and deep bond. But this intensity is deceptive. It's not about a real connection that naturally develops and grows, but about a calculated move to destabilize and gain power. Every gesture and every word is part of a strategy to manipulate emotions and create a false sense of security.

That's why love bombing is so difficult to recognize at first: it exploits the same emotions we seek in authentic love—feeling special, desired, loved. But in love bombing, these emotions are not the goal but the means. They are not the manifestation of a genuine feeling but the bait to draw the other into the net. And when the prey is caught, the seemingly overwhelming love begins to show its true face: control.

In love, vulnerability is an act of courage, a gift that two people give each other to grow together. But in love bombing, the other person's vulnerability becomes an opportunity to manipulate. While authentic love respects time, growth, and distance, love bombing rushes because it knows that if it stopped, if it slowed down, its true intentions might be uncovered.

Recognizing the Signs: When It's Too Good to Be True

Recognizing love bombing can be challenging, especially because, on the surface, it can seem like the start of a dream romance. However, there are specific signs that, once understood, can help you distinguish between authentic love and manipulation disguised as affection. Here are some of the most common signs to look out for:

1. **Rushed Intimacy**

   The love bomber tends to speed through milestones. Early in the relationship, you may find yourself involved in deeply personal conversations, with premature declarations of love and proposals to live together or make long-term plans after just a few dates. This unnatural acceleration is designed to create a rapid and intense emotional connection, leaving you feeling like you can't live without the other person.

2. **Managing Your Emotions**

   If your partner constantly tries to influence or direct how you should feel, it's a red flag. Phrases like "Don't be sad, I'm here for you" or "You don't need to worry about anything, I'll take care of everything" may seem reassuring but actually minimize your feelings and your need to express them authentically. A healthy partner leaves space for you to feel and deal with your emotions instead of trying to manage or control them.

3. Excessive Compliments

While everyone appreciates compliments, a constant and disproportionate flow of praise can be a sign of love bombing. Comments like "You're the most incredible person I've ever met," "I've never felt anything like this before," or "No one has ever understood me like you do" repeated continuously may seem flattering, but they are often tactics to build emotional dependency, making you crave those confirmations more and more.

4. Ostentatious and Unexpected Generosity

The love bomber often uses extravagant gifts or unexpected generous gestures as a means to impress and bind the other person to them. It could be expensive gifts, grand surprises, or an excessive amount of attention that seems almost disproportionate to the level of mutual acquaintance. This generosity, rather than being a sign of genuine affection, is intended to create a sense of debt or obligation.

5. Disrespect for Personal Boundaries

A sign of love bombing is the partner's refusal or difficulty in respecting your personal boundaries. They may push you to spend all your time with them, ignoring or minimizing your other relationships and activities. They may become jealous or possessive if you spend time with friends or family, trying to make you feel guilty for not putting them first.

6. **Sudden Emotional Fluctuations**

Another red flag is a sudden and dramatic change in levels of affection or attention. At first, you may feel like the center of their universe, only to be suddenly ignored or treated coldly. These fluctuations are designed to keep you in a state of emotional confusion, always searching for the next affectionate gesture.

7. **Pressure to Make Quick, Committing Decisions**

The love bomber often pushes you to make important decisions before you're ready: moving in together, changing cities, quitting a job, or distancing yourself from friends and family. This rush is meant to prevent you from having the time to reflect and realize how the relationship is becoming oppressive or harmful.

8. **Progressive Isolation from Loved Ones**

If you notice your social circle shrinking and your partner discouraging you from seeing or talking to friends and family, it's a worrying sign. The love bomber may do this subtly, perhaps insinuating that certain people don't really understand you or don't have your best interests at heart, creating a sense of dependency on them.

9. **Use of Guilt and Shame**

    A love bomber often uses guilt as a tool for manipulation. They may make you feel guilty for not responding to their messages right away or for not immediately reciprocating the same amount of affection and attention they give you. Or they might make you feel ashamed for your emotions or desire for personal space, labeling your needs as "selfish" or "insensitive."

10. **Inconsistency Between Words and Actions**

    Finally, one of the most evident signs is the discrepancy between what the partner says and what they do. Promises and declarations of love that don't align with daily actions, sudden attitude changes, or contradictions between what they say they want and how they behave are clear indicators of manipulative behavior.

Final Reflection

If your answers lean toward "too much," "reacts negatively," "minimizes," "under pressure," or "modified," you might want to explore further whether there are control or manipulation dynamics in your relationship. Every relationship is unique and complex; if you have doubts, consider speaking with a counselor for a professional perspective.

Chapter 2: The Stages of Love Bombing

Love bombing is a journey that begins with an explosion of affection, a whirlwind race toward ideal love, but soon reveals its darker side. It is a dynamic that unfolds in different stages, each with its distinct traits, designed to create, strengthen, and then solidify a bond based on manipulation and control.

In the early stages, everything seems perfect, almost as if we've finally found the right person, the soulmate who completes us in every way. This is the phase of **the idyll**, where everything seems too good to be true, because it often is. This seemingly magical moment is designed to emotionally disarm us, to lower our defenses and allow the other to deeply insinuate themselves into our lives.

But soon, the idyll transforms into something different.

The phase of **control** begins, a time when the affection and attention that once seemed limitless begin to be used as tools of power. Personal boundaries are tested, and individual freedom gradually shrinks. Love becomes oppressive, suffocating, and what once seemed like a promise of happiness turns into a gilded cage.

Finally, the phase of **devaluation and emotional blackmail** emerges. The love that once seemed unconditional becomes a bargaining chip, a tool for manipulation and control. The same affectionate gestures that wrapped us in a warm blanket of security now serve to threaten, blackmail, and keep the victim in a constant state of insecurity and dependency.

In this chapter, we will explore these three stages of love bombing in detail, helping you recognize them, understand how they work, and learn how to protect yourself from this type of emotional manipulation.

The Phase of the Idyll: How It Manifests

The phase of the idyll is the seductive beginning of love bombing, what we might call "the accelerated honeymoon." In this stage, everything appears perfect, almost as if taken from a romantic movie. It's the moment when the love bomber puts on a show of seemingly unconditional love and affection, but one that actually hides a manipulative intent.

This phase manifests through a cascade of gestures and words aimed at making the other person feel special, unique, and irreplaceable. It's a continuous emotional assault, designed to break down defenses and create an immediate and deep bond. But how can you tell when something that seems wonderful is actually a trap?

Premature and Overwhelming Declarations of Love

During the idyll, the love bomber does not hesitate to declare their love almost instantly. You might hear phrases like, *"You're the love of my life," "I've never met anyone like you,"* or *"I know we are meant to be together."* These words, spoken too early, often within the first few weeks of a relationship, are designed to create a sense of euphoria and uniqueness. The idea is to make you feel like you are the center of their world, the answer to all their prayers.

Grand and Exaggerated Gestures

Expensive gifts, unexpected surprises, romantic weekends planned with almost manic care: the love bomber uses these gestures to impress you and make you feel safe. These acts of generosity may seem sincere, but often they are disproportionate to the length and depth of the relationship. The goal is to make you believe you are so special that you deserve such intense and extraordinary love, creating a kind of emotional dependency on these gestures.

Constant and Intrusive Attention

In the idyll phase, attention is constant, almost obsessive. The love bomber bombards you with messages, calls, emails, and social media posts, wanting to always be present, constantly involved in every aspect of your life. They wake you up with a "good morning" text, wish you "good night," and make sure every moment in between is filled with them. At first glance, this might seem romantic, but the intensity is no accident: it serves to fill every emotional void in your life, reducing your ability to reflect on the relationship objectively.

Creation of a Private and Exclusive World

The love bomber tends to isolate the partner in an exclusive world, made up of just the two of you. Initially, it may seem like a beautiful intimacy: evenings spent talking for hours, shared confidences that you've never told anyone else, promises of a perfect future together. But this exclusivity is designed to gradually distance you from friends and family, creating an emotional dependency where the other becomes your only point of reference.

Building a Fairytale Narrative

During the idyll, the love bomber might construct an idealized narrative of your relationship, telling your story as if it were fate written in the stars. Words like *"it was love at first sight"* or *"I know you're my soulmate"* are common. They paint you as the only person who has ever truly understood their soul, elevating a special connection that seems beyond anything you've ever experienced. This type of rhetoric creates a kind of romantic myth around the relationship, an illusion of perfection that makes it difficult to see beyond.

Incessant Compliments and Endless Flattery

The love bomber inundates you with compliments: *"You're perfect," "No one has ever made me feel like this," "There's no one like you."* These compliments, repeated incessantly, may seem sincere and put you on a pedestal. But they are often tools to make the victim constantly crave that type of confirmation and attention, creating an emotional dependency based on the need for continuous approval.

Reinforcement of Bonds with Immediate and Sudden Gestures

In this phase, you may find yourself involved in immediate gestures, such as being given a house key or discussing marriage or children after just a few weeks. You may perceive that decisions that would normally take time are being made with surprising, almost forced speed. This serves to create a false sense of stability and security, anchoring you in the relationship before you've had time to reflect.

Avoidance of Deep and Meaningful Discussions

While everything seems wonderful, you may notice that the love bomber avoids discussing serious or difficult topics. If you try to bring up a doubt or concern, they tend to minimize, change the subject, or immediately return to praise and romantic gestures. The intent is clear: to keep you in the idyll phase as long as possible, without ever confronting reality or any problems that may arise.

The Appeal of the Emotional Honeymoon

The idyll phase of love bombing is often compared to an "emotional honeymoon," a period when everything seems perfect, and emotions are at their peak. But what makes it particularly seductive is how it plays with our deep, often unconscious, desires. Many of us are conditioned to believe in "movie-style" love stories, where love is instant, passionate, and overwhelming. The love bomber knows how to exploit this imagery, built over years of romantic comedies, romance novels, and childhood fairytales.

But there's an interesting psychological phenomenon to consider: the effect of **the "soulmate dream."** This term describes the tendency to romanticize and idealize relationships, especially those that seem to spring up suddenly and magically. Psychological studies have shown that people often perceive relationships that begin with a "love at first sight" moment as more authentic or destined to last. This is because our brain associates the intensity of initial emotions with a sort of "guarantee" of the authenticity of the feeling.

The love bomber uses this very mechanism: creating a reality that seems to confirm the narrative of the "predestined connection," knowing that those who believe in it will be more inclined to ignore red flags and remain in the relationship, even when things start to turn negative.

The Science of Immediate Infatuation

During the idyll phase, our brain is literally flooded with chemicals — dopamine, serotonin, and oxytocin — that make us feel euphoric and bonded to the other person. These substances create a sort of "biochemical cocktail" that transports us on an emotional rollercoaster, where every gesture or word from the love bomber seems to amplify our feelings. But, as with any chemically-induced "high," there are side effects: critical thinking diminishes, and we become more vulnerable to believing that what we're experiencing is unique and unrepeatable.

To better understand this phenomenon, let's take a closer look at the substances involved:

- **Dopamine:** Often called the "reward molecule," dopamine is responsible for the feeling of pleasure we experience when something positive happens. In the context of love bombing, every compliment, affectionate message, or romantic gesture triggers a rush of dopamine, creating an immediate and gratifying sensation of pleasure. This reward cycle drives us to crave more of those "special moments," making us more susceptible to manipulation. When the love bomber inundates us with attention, our brain interprets these signals as rewards, creating a dependency similar to what we experience with gambling or substance use.

- **Serotonin:** During the idyll phase, serotonin levels – a neurotransmitter that regulates mood, sleep, and appetite – can drop dramatically. This decrease occurs because the brain becomes hyper-focused on the object of desire, which can lead to a form of obsession. In other words, intense infatuation often manifests with constant, intrusive thoughts about the loved one, similar to what occurs in obsessive-compulsive disorder (OCD). The love bomber exploits this altered mental state to keep you in a constant state of emotional agitation and attachment.

- **Oxytocin:** Also known as "the love hormone" or "the bonding hormone," oxytocin is released in large quantities during moments of physical or emotional intimacy. Every hug, kiss, or deep connection stimulates the release of oxytocin, creating a chemical bond that reinforces the feeling of closeness and affection. However, when the love bomber uses oxytocin as a tool, each moment of physical closeness becomes a way to strengthen the emotional bond and make it almost unbreakable, even if the relationship is toxic.

The Tunnel Vision of Passion

During this phase, you might experience what psychologists call **the "passion tunnel vision."** When we're in love or infatuated, our brain can narrow our ability to see the situation objectively. This phenomenon is amplified by the constant presence of dopamine and oxytocin, which make us focus only on the positive qualities of the other person, completely ignoring warning signs.

The "tunnel vision" makes it difficult to listen to our inner voice, that part of us that might have doubts or notice inconsistencies. It's as if the brain itself constructs a filter that discards any information that contradicts the romantic narrative we've created in our mind. During love bombing, this tunnel tightens even more, making it harder to perceive the manipulative behavior of the other person.

The Emotional Sugar Crash

Love bombing works like a diet made of **"emotional sugar"**: at first, everything is sweet and gratifying, but in the long term, the lack of real emotional nutrients can cause an internal crisis. The brain, accustomed to a constant flow of dopamine, serotonin, and oxytocin, can become increasingly dependent on these "hits" to feel good. However, when these chemicals start to fade — as inevitably happens when the love bomber shifts to the control or devaluation phase — you may experience a sort of "emotional withdrawal," similar to that of a substance addiction.

This phase is marked by anxiety, depression, confusion, and a sense of emptiness. The victim may feel driven to do anything to return to those initial moments of euphoria, making them even more vulnerable to the manipulations and control of the love bomber. It's a subtle and powerful trap: the desire to return to that first period of "perfection" is precisely what keeps the victim hooked on the toxic relationship.

Understanding the Game of Emotional Chemistry

Knowing that the chemical reactions in your brain play a huge role during the idyll phase allows you to see beyond the initial euphoria and excitement. Remember, these feelings are not necessarily indicators of authentic love, but could be the result of a "chemical cocktail" designed to create emotional dependency. Being aware of your physical and emotional reactions is the first step to avoiding falling into an emotional trap constructed with intent. When you feel that the intensity is building too quickly, take a moment to reflect and ask yourself: "Is this connection really real, or is it just a reaction to the chemicals in my brain?"

The Control Phase: When Love Becomes Oppressive

After the idyll phase, where everything seemed perfect and overwhelming, love bombing enters a new phase: **the phase of control.** At this point, the atmosphere gradually changes. The partner who once showered you with attention and affection begins to shrink your space for freedom, turning what seemed like love into a form of oppression.

The control phase manifests through a series of behaviors aimed at reducing your autonomy, making you increasingly dependent on the love bomber. This change is often subtle and progressive, passing almost unnoticed, until you find yourself feeling trapped without knowing how you got there.

Limitation of Personal Independence

One of the first signs of the control phase is the gradual limitation of your autonomy. The love bomber might start insisting on how you should organize your time, pushing you to reduce or eliminate activities you once enjoyed in favor of spending more time with them. They might ask you to give up hobbies, interests, or even work, justifying it with phrases like "so we can spend more time together" or "I'm just trying to protect our love." Little by little, you find yourself becoming more dependent on their choices and losing control over your life.

Continuous and Invasive Monitoring

The love bomber begins to constantly monitor your actions. They may want to know where you are, who you're with, and what you're doing at all times, presenting this request as a form of concern or love. They might insist on reading your messages, checking your calls, or even asking you to continuously share your location through tracking apps. This behavior is disguised as a desire to protect you, but in reality, it is a way to exercise constant control over you and limit your personal freedom.

Social and Emotional Isolation

Another clear sign of the control phase is the gradual isolation from the people you care about. The love bomber may begin to belittle your friends or family, insinuating that they don't really understand you or don't have your best interests at heart. Phrases like "Your friends don't understand you like I do" or "Your parents are too intrusive, they don't get our love" become increasingly common. These comments, seemingly harmless, are designed to distance you from your support networks and make you more emotionally dependent on them.

Jealousy and Emotional Control

Jealousy is one of the main weapons used during this phase. The love bomber may start showing signs of jealousy, demanding explanations for every interaction you have with other people, even when there are no obvious reasons. Phrases like "I'm jealous because I love you so much" or "I just worry about you" become a way to justify increasingly intrusive demands for control. This seemingly innocent jealousy hides a deeper need to exercise power and create an environment where the love bomber is the center of your attention.

Manipulation Through "Caring"

During this phase, control may be disguised as excessive caring or "advice" that seems to come from a place of love. The love bomber might tell you they "only want what's best for you," subtly criticizing your choices and insinuating that you should do things differently. For example, they might say: "I don't understand why you want to do that, it's not safe" or "It really isn't good for you to spend time with those people, they don't help you." These seemingly loving suggestions are actually attempts to manipulate you into feeling obliged to follow their advice, further undermining your independence.

Creating Emotional Dependency

A key goal of this phase is to create emotional dependency. The love bomber will try to position themselves as the only person you need, your only emotional support. They might lower your self-esteem with subtle comments or veiled criticisms, making you believe that no one else would accept or love you as they do. In this way, even when you feel oppressed or suffocated, you'll be afraid to leave, believing that no one else could ever offer you what they do.

Pressure to Conform to Their Expectations

Finally, during this phase, the love bomber begins to apply pressure for you to conform to their expectations, attempting to mold you into their ideal vision. They may tell you how to dress, how to behave, what interests to pursue, and which people you should associate with. The love that once seemed unconditional now becomes conditioned on your compliance with their desires. Any act of rebellion or difference is seen as a threat to the relationship, fostering an atmosphere of tension and control.

The Mechanism of "Gaslighting"

One of the most powerful tools used during the control phase is **gaslighting**, a form of psychological manipulation that aims to make you doubt your perception of reality. The term comes from the 1944 film *Gaslight*, in which a husband manipulates his wife into believing she is going insane by gradually dimming the gas lights in their home and denying that the lights have changed when she notices.

In the context of love bombing, gaslighting manifests when the love bomber begins to question your memory, feelings, or perception of events. For example, you might hear phrases like, "Do you really think that happened like that? You're getting confused," "You're too sensitive, you're overreacting," or "I never said that, you're making it up." These comments are designed to make you feel insecure and confused about your perception of reality.

Why Does Gaslighting Work?

Gaslighting is effective because it slowly infiltrates your mind, playing on the trust you place in the other person and your ability to judge situations. Initially, you might think these are simple misunderstandings, but over time, the accumulation of these episodes makes you start doubting yourself and your mental stability. It's an attack on your self-esteem and inner confidence, making you increasingly dependent on the other person for a "correct" version of reality.

How to Recognize Gaslighting

Gaslighting often accompanies a feeling of disorientation or confusion. If you find yourself frequently wondering if you truly misunderstood something, if you've exaggerated a situation, or if you're "losing your mind," it could be a sign that you're being manipulated in this way. It's important to trust your instincts and your perceptions: if something feels wrong, it probably is.

The Importance of Awareness
Being aware of this manipulation tactic is the first step to countering it. The key to defending yourself against gaslighting is to stay anchored to your own reality, maintain an external support network (such as friends and family who can help you verify facts), and, if necessary, seek support from a therapist or counselor. Recognizing that the problem isn't you, but rather the other person's attempt to exert control, will give you the strength to resist this subtle manipulation.

The Devaluation and Emotional Blackmail Phase: When Love Becomes a Bargaining Chip

After establishing emotional control and limiting your independence, the love bomber enters an even darker and more painful phase: **the phase of devaluation and emotional blackmail**. If, during the control phase, the partner sought to maintain subtle dominance through manipulation and restrictions, in this phase, the game becomes more aggressive. The love that once seemed so generous and unconditional now turns into a true bargaining chip, used to manipulate, intimidate, and keep you in a state of constant insecurity.

This phase is characterized by an alternation of devaluation and emotional promises that leave the victim confused, anxious, and constantly seeking approval. It's a cycle that, if not interrupted, can lead to severe psychological damage and the loss of self-esteem.

Devaluation and Continuous Criticism

One of the most obvious aspects of this phase is systematic devaluation. What was once presented as unconditional love turns into a series of criticisms and negative comments. The love bomber begins to undermine your self-esteem with phrases like, "You're too sensitive," "You're not good enough at this," or "No one will ever love you like I do." These statements are aimed at making you feel inadequate and insecure, planting the seed that you're not worthy of love outside the relationship.

The criticisms can target any aspect of your person: from your physical appearance, to your intelligence, to how you behave or speak. The goal is to destroy your confidence in yourself, making you more and more dependent on the love bomber's approval as the only one who "tolerates" or "accepts" who you truly are.

Alternation Between Devaluation and False Reassurances

The love bomber doesn't devalue you constantly: they alternate criticism with brief moments of reassurance. After attacking or criticizing you, they may offer a sudden gesture of affection, like an unexpected compliment or a gift. This oscillation between devaluation and false reassurance creates a psychological effect known as **"intermittent reinforcement,"** which is one of the most powerful methods of creating emotional dependency.

These small acts of kindness, interspersed between criticisms, keep you in a state of waiting, hoping that the negative phase will end and the affection from the past will return. It's a dynamic similar to that seen in gambling addiction: you never know when the next positive moment will come, so you remain hooked, hoping for change.

Emotional Blackmail: Love as a Weapon of Control
The love bomber uses affection as a bargaining chip, turning love into a weapon of control. You might hear phrases like: *"If you really loved me, you'd do this for me," "After everything I've done for you, how can you refuse?"* or *"You're the one forcing me to behave this way."* These phrases are designed to make you feel guilty, making you believe that every problem or difficulty in the relationship is your fault and that your love is constantly being tested.

Emotional blackmail becomes a subtle but devastating form of control. Every gesture, every word, every decision is filtered through this dynamic where love is conditional on your complete compliance and obedience. You find yourself walking on eggshells, constantly trying not to disappoint, not to do anything that might anger or upset the love bomber.

Emotional Punishments and Withdrawal of Affection

In this phase, the love bomber also uses the withdrawal of affection as a form of punishment. They may suddenly become cold, distant, or stop communicating without explanation. You may find yourself emotionally excluded, faced with a "wall of silence" that seems insurmountable. This withdrawal of affection is often preceded by episodes of anger or frustration, leaving you wondering what you did wrong.

Emotional punishments can also take the form of subtle threats, like "I don't know how I could go on without you," or more explicit ones, like "If you leave, you'll ruin everything we've built." These threats play on the fear of losing everything you've built in the relationship, preying on your fear of abandonment and isolation.

Devaluation of Your Personal Worth

The love bomber begins to erode your perception of your own value. They might belittle your qualities, ridicule your passions, or downplay your successes. Phrases like *"You're lucky I'm with you; no one else would put up with you"* or *"You'd be nothing without me"* become common. This continuous devaluation is meant to make you believe that you have no worth outside of the relationship, that no one else could ever love or accept you the way the love bomber does.

Manipulation Through Guilt

The love bomber often resorts to guilt as a means of manipulation. Anytime you try to set boundaries or express your needs, you are accused of being selfish, insensitive, or ungrateful. You might hear things like, *"After everything I've done for you, you act like this?"* or *"You're so selfish, you only think of yourself."* This type of manipulation keeps you feeling perpetually at fault, forcing you to justify your feelings and choices.

Creation of a Climate of Fear and Insecurity

The love bomber creates a constant atmosphere of insecurity, where you never know what to expect. You may fear their reactions, worry about every word or gesture, and live in a state of perpetual emotional tension. This fear drives you to constantly seek their approval, doing everything you can to avoid conflict or displeasure. Your life becomes a continuous struggle to maintain balance, to not trigger negative reactions, and to earn the affection that is granted to you sparingly.

Victimization as a Final Weapon

In this phase, the love bomber may often assume the role of the victim to manipulate you further. They might constantly complain about how misunderstood, lonely, or neglected they feel, insinuating that you don't love them enough or aren't doing enough to show your affection. Phrases like *"I don't know how I'll manage without you," "If you leave, you'll ruin my life,"* or *"I'm so unhappy without you"* are common. This tactic plays on your empathy and sense of guilt, making it increasingly difficult for you to distance yourself or make decisions that are healthy for you.

The "False Hope" and the Cycle of Emotional Abuse

Before we dive into the next chapter, where we'll explore the psychological profile of the love bomber, it's crucial to reflect on a key element: **"false hope."** This concept represents a devastating illusion, an unfulfilled promise that the manipulative partner intentionally nurtures to keep the victim trapped in the relationship.

"False hope" manifests as the belief that, if only you could do enough, love enough, or prove your worth, everything could magically return to the happy days at the beginning of the relationship when love seemed authentic and perfect. This illusion feeds on the victim's vulnerability and deepest emotions, making them cling to the idea that with the right effort, it's possible to reclaim that ideal love.

The Cycle of Emotional Abuse

"False hope" doesn't exist in a vacuum but is part of a broader phenomenon known as the **cycle of emotional abuse.** This cycle includes three main stages that repeat over time:

1. **Rising Tension:** In this phase, the manipulative partner becomes increasingly irritable, critical, and distant. The victim senses a tense atmosphere and desperately tries to "do everything right" to maintain peace.

2. **Explosion:** After a period of rising tension, the manipulator snaps. The explosion can take the form of violent arguments, unfounded accusations, or emotionally abusive behaviors. At this moment, the victim is often blamed for everything that's wrong in the relationship and is manipulated with guilt, emotional punishments, or veiled threats.

3. **"Honeymoon" or Reconciliation:** Following the explosion, the manipulator may show signs of remorse, regret, and sudden affection. Promises of change, seemingly sincere apologies, and gestures of love reignite the victim's hope that things could get better. This is where "false hope" becomes especially powerful: the victim, seeking relief from emotional suffering, clings to these promises, hoping that this time things will be different.

Why Is the Cycle of Emotional Abuse So Effective?

The cycle of tension-explosion-reconciliation creates a devastating dynamic, trapping the victim between the fear of loss and the illusion of reconciliation. Each time the "honeymoon phase" reappears, even if brief and fleeting, it reinforces emotional dependency. The love bomber uses this "false hope" as an emotional trap, knowing that the victim, in their vulnerability and desire to recover lost love, will be willing to endure even the abuse, just to relive those moments of reprieve and apparent affection.

"False hope" is, therefore, a powerful and insidious tool of control, prolonging the victim's suffering and keeping them in a relationship that was never truly authentic.

Chapter 3: Who Is the Love Bomber?

When we think about who might use love bombing, it's easy to imagine a figure with clearly defined, almost "villainous" traits like someone from a romantic movie. However, the reality is much more complex and nuanced. The love bomber doesn't always present themselves with a sinister look or the appearance of someone scheming in the shadows. On the contrary, they often hide behind the face of someone who seems genuinely in love, affectionate, and caring—someone who seems too good to be true, because, in a sense, they are.

In this chapter, we'll dive into the psychological profiles of those who resort to love bombing, exploring the different personality types that can adopt this manipulative strategy. We'll discuss narcissists, manipulators, and other toxic personalities who, for various reasons, choose to use love as a mask to hide their true intentions.

But we won't stop at just describing these profiles. We'll seek to understand the motivations that drive them to act this way, exploring the psychological and emotional reasons that lead them to see relationships not as a space for mutual growth, but as a playing field to conquer, where manipulation and control become the main rules.

We will also explore the most common behavioral patterns these individuals use to trap their victims. How can you recognize them? What are the warning signs that someone might be a love bomber? These are the questions we'll try to answer, providing practical tools to distinguish between sincere love and an emotional trap.

But before we begin, let me say this: not everyone who shows intense signs of affection is necessarily a manipulator or abuser. However, understanding the dynamics that fuel love bombing and who practices it can make the difference between making informed choices and falling into a spiral of suffering and confusion.

Psychological Profiles: Narcissists, Manipulators, and Toxic Personalities

To fully understand who the love bomber is, it's essential to explore the psychological profiles that often resort to this manipulative tactic. These individuals are not a homogeneous group; they have different motivations and emotional dynamics that drive them to use love as a tool of control. However, there are some common traits we can identify to help us recognize their behavior before it becomes a problem.

1. **The Narcissist: Love as a Reflection of Themselves**

    The narcissist is perhaps the most well-known profile associated with love bombing, but that doesn't make them any less complex or predictable. At the heart of narcissistic behavior is a deep and insatiable need for admiration, a desire to be seen and appreciated as superior, special, unique. For the narcissist, love is not a reciprocal exchange of feelings, but a mirror in which they see their idealized image reflected. Every relationship becomes a kind of stage, where the other is relegated to the role of spectator or supporter.

    These individuals often appear charming, charismatic, and seductive. They can capture others' attention and interest with disarming ease, making their partner feel as though they're the only one in the world. Their talent for flattery may seem genuine: generous compliments, excessive romantic gestures, and overwhelming declarations of love are part of the package. But the true goal is to conquer and validate themselves, not the other. Love bombing becomes a strategy to gain the attention and adoration they need to feel important and superior.

The Inner Void of the Narcissist

Behind the facade of confidence, the narcissist hides an inner void, a sense of inadequacy they try to fill through others' adoration. They have a fragile self-esteem that depends entirely on how they're perceived and treated by those around them. This is why the narcissist must always be the center of attention, praised, and admired. When the partner satisfies this need, the narcissist responds with grandiose and generous gestures of love. But when admiration wanes or is insufficient, the facade falls, and their true face emerges.

From Seduction to Contempt

For the narcissist, love bombing is only the first act of a longer performance. Once the narcissist has obtained the desired confirmation and feels secure in the relationship, they can quickly lose interest. Constant attention and adoration are never enough, and the partner becomes "boring" or "inadequate" if they fail to maintain that level of gratification. At this point, the narcissist can become distant, cold, or even aggressive. Often, this change happens suddenly and inexplicably, leaving the partner confused and hurt, always searching for what they did wrong.

When the partner tries to establish boundaries or express emotional needs, the narcissist may react with anger or disdain. To them, any request for reciprocity or empathy is perceived as a personal attack or a sign of weakness in the other, and they respond by devaluing the partner to reaffirm their superiority. This devaluation can manifest in biting criticisms, ridicule, or even public humiliation.

The Narcissist's "Mask"

The narcissist is highly skilled at maintaining a "mask" of perfection and charisma in public, while in private they may show completely different behavior. They're often well-liked and respected, able to impress colleagues, friends, and even family members with their charm and apparent confidence. However, behind the scenes, this mask can easily fall when they fail to receive the level of attention and respect they believe they deserve. This dichotomy can further confuse the partner, who struggles to explain the true nature of the person they're living with. The narcissist can use their social status or public charm to manipulate the situation further, making the partner appear to be the problem or someone who "doesn't understand."

How to Recognize Them:

- **Excessive need for attention and praise:** The narcissist constantly seeks to be the center of attention, craving compliments and recognition. They feed off others' admiration and actively pursue it.

- **Manipulative behaviors to gain admiration:** They use tactics like love bombing, heroic tales about themselves, or even lies to paint themselves as extraordinary and indispensable.

- **Tendency to devalue others:** When they no longer receive the desired admiration, they may shift from praise to criticism, devaluing the other to reaffirm their sense of superiority.

- **Lack of empathy:** The narcissist has difficulty feeling genuine empathy for others' feelings and needs. Even when they seem to understand emotionally, it's only to manipulate or take advantage of the situation.

Subtle Warning Signs:

- **Exaggerated reactions to rejection or criticism:** Even a mild hint of criticism can trigger a disproportionate reaction, revealing hidden vulnerability.

- **Constant need for self-celebration:** The narcissist frequently talks about themselves, their achievements, and expects others to do the same.

- **Inability to maintain stable relationships:** Their relationships often start with intense passion but end abruptly when the other person stops being "useful" as a source of adoration.

2. The Manipulator: Love as a Tool of Power

The manipulator is another psychological profile often associated with love bombing, but their motivations and methods differ significantly from those of the narcissist. While the narcissist seeks adoration and validation, the manipulator is driven by the need for control. For them, love is a tool, a means to an end, which often involves power and domination over others. Love bombing becomes a tactic to establish emotional and psychological dominance over the partner.

The Manipulator and the Game of Power

The manipulator uses love bombing as a weapon, approaching with affection and care one moment, only to become suddenly cold and distant the next. This alternation between affectionate and detached behaviors creates a constant atmosphere of uncertainty, keeping the victim in a state of continuous emotional tension. The partner is left striving to "earn back" the lost affection, often without understanding how or why it was withdrawn in the first place. This keeps the victim in a weakened position, always seeking approval.

The Illusion of Benevolent Control

The manipulator is a master of seduction and emotional manipulation. They can adapt their behavior and language according to the victim's reactions, adjusting their attitude to get what they want. One of their favorite tactics is to create an illusion of **benevolent control**: they might appear caring and protective, making the other person feel loved and safe. Phrases like *"I'm doing this just to protect you"* or *"I worry about you"* are common. But behind these words, the real goal is to make the victim completely dependent on them, believing that only the manipulator knows what's best for them.

The manipulator knows how to build grand dreams and promises, painting a perfect future that seems within reach. They might talk about a life together, fantastic plans, endless happiness. But these promises are made to keep the victim emotionally hooked and can be withdrawn in a heartbeat if the manipulator feels their control is threatened. This constant process of giving and taking leaves the victim confused and dependent, desperately trying to reclaim what was promised.

Manipulator Tactics: Alternation and Emotional Uncertainty

The manipulator uses a combination of techniques to maintain control:

- **Affection and praise followed by distance and**

coldness: One day, they might shower you with compliments, telling you that you're the only person they've ever truly loved, and the next day, they may suddenly become cold and distant, ignoring your messages or treating you with disdain. This alternation creates emotional confusion, leaving you feeling as if you're always in the wrong, trying to figure out what you did to cause the change. The victim is constantly engaged in trying to earn back the lost affection, fueling the manipulator's power.

- **Manipulation through fear and guilt:** The manipulator is an expert at using fear and guilt as control mechanisms. They might tell you that without them, your life would be empty, or that you're ungrateful for everything they've done for you. Phrases like "If you leave me, you'll be alone forever" or "After all I've sacrificed for you, how can you treat me like this?" are used to instill insecurity and guilt, making you feel responsible for their emotional well-being.

- **Minimizing or denying their own responsibilities:** Another common tactic is to minimize or deny their own responsibilities when confronted. If accused of manipulative or inappropriate behavior, the manipulator may deflect attention, change the subject, or worse, reverse the roles, making the victim seem like the real aggressor. Phrases like "You're overreacting" or "You're too sensitive" are used to devalue the other person's feelings and make them feel irrational or paranoid.

The "Mask of Affection" of the Manipulator

The manipulator knows how to maintain a mask of affection and care in public or in moments where they perceive that their control is at risk. They may seem like the perfect, attentive, and devoted lover, especially when there are witnesses or when an external threat could break the relationship. This behavior makes it difficult for the victim to explain their torment to others, as the manipulator appears outwardly impeccable, loving, and attentive.

How to Recognize Them:

- **Alternation between extreme affection and sudden distance:** The manipulator frequently shifts between being affectionate and caring to cold and distant, keeping the victim in a constant state of emotional uncertainty.

- **Emotional manipulation to induce guilt or fear:** They use fear and guilt to control the partner, often resorting to subtle threats or statements that create insecurity.

- **Minimizing or denying responsibilities:** When challenged or accused of wrongdoings, the manipulator tends to minimize their actions, deny them, or shift the blame onto the other person.

- **Ability to quickly adapt:** They can modify their behavior and words based on the other person's reactions, always seeking to maintain emotional and psychological control.

Subtle Warning Signs:

- **Unrealistic promises and dreams:** The manipulator often paints an idyllic future that never seems to materialize, using these dreams to keep the other hooked.

- **Unpredictable reactions:** They change moods quickly and seemingly without reason, leaving the other unsure of how to behave.

- **Gradual isolation:** Like the narcissist, the manipulator may attempt to isolate the victim, but they do so more subtly, using genuine-seeming concerns or care to justify distancing them from friends or family.

3. The Toxic Personality: Love as a Strategy Game

The toxic personality is a complex, elusive profile, often difficult to identify because it combines elements of narcissism, manipulation, and other dysfunctional dynamics. These individuals see relationships not as a place for growth and authentic connection but as a playing field where they exercise power, experience intense emotions, or simply fill an inner void. For them, love bombing is a strategy not so much to keep a partner close, but to maintain control of the dynamic itself, using love as a pawn in a bigger game.

The Game of Power and Chaos

These toxic personalities are often drawn to intense and unstable relationships because they feed off the chaos these situations generate. Drama, conflict, and emotional instability are part of their daily life, and they even seem to actively seek these elements. For them, emotion is life, even if it's negative or painful. A stable and calm relationship is seen as boring, meaningless. Therefore, they create situations where the other person is always "on edge," uncertain of what will happen next.

The Emotional Chameleon

Toxic personalities are highly skilled at changing their mask depending on the circumstances. They can be sweet and loving one day, and cruel and distant the next. This contradictory behavior serves to keep the other person in a state of constant emotional confusion, ensuring that the partner is always uncertain of what to expect and, as a result, easier to manipulate. These individuals can quickly switch from being caring to manipulative, from affectionate to critical, from passionate to indifferent, all depending on what they find most useful at a given moment.

Love as a Challenge and Manipulation

For the toxic personality, love bombing is a challenge: they can seduce, conquer, and then destabilize, only to repeat the cycle. They use lies, half-truths, and manipulations to keep the partner hooked, always uncertain about the "truth" of the relationship. This creates an atmosphere of instability that works to their advantage, as the partner is constantly trying to figure out what's happening, rather than focusing on their own needs or happiness.

How to Recognize Them:

- **Unpredictable and contradictory behaviors:** They frequently change moods and attitudes without apparent reason, creating a constant atmosphere of uncertainty.

- **Tendency to create conflicts and drama:** They actively seek situations of tension and conflict to keep the focus on themselves and feed the drama in the relationship.

- **Use of lies and manipulations:** They often tell half-truths or inconsistent stories to keep the partner confused and uncertain.

- **Alternation between sweetness and cruelty:** They can be incredibly affectionate and kind one day, and then suddenly become critical, distant, or even hostile.

Subtle Warning Signs:

- **Inconsistency in their stories or accounts:** They change versions of events or their experiences depending on the circumstances.

- **Creation of relational triangles:** They often involve other people (exes, friends, colleagues) to create situations of jealousy or competition.

- **Manipulation of reality:** They make you doubt your perception of events, causing you to question your own experiences.

4. The "Savior": Love as a Need for Redemption

The "savior" represents another complex and less obvious profile of the love bomber. This type of individual is driven by a deep desire to feel needed or indispensable. They want to be seen as the hero, the martyr, or the "rescuer" in the situation. Unlike other profiles that use love bombing to gain power or direct control, the "savior" seeks to create emotional dependency based on the need for help and support.

Deceptive Altruism

At first, the "savior" may appear incredibly caring and altruistic. They offer support, assistance, and unconditional love, making their partner feel loved and protected. But this generosity is often a means to obtain personal gratification. In reality, what the "savior" wants is for their partner to feel incapable of handling life without them, creating a bond of dependency. Every act of altruism hides a subtle manipulation: the other person must feel weak, needy, and grateful for being "saved."

Creating Emotional Dependency

The "savior" excels at building a narrative where they appear as the only person who can truly help or understand you. At first, they may seem like the ideal partner: always available, always ready to solve your problems. But over time, their generosity becomes suffocating. They might insist on doing things for you that you never asked for or offer help in situations where it's not needed, making you feel incapable or powerless. Every time you try to take control of your life or assert your independence, the "savior" may react with frustration or resentment, seeing your autonomy as a threat to their identity as the "martyr."

Heroism as Control

The "savior" uses their apparent generosity as a tool of control. They do everything possible to create situations where the other person seems weak or in difficulty, only to step in and "save the day." This cycle reinforces the idea that only they can help or truly understand you. They may also adopt a morally superior attitude, emphasizing how much they are sacrificing for you, making you feel guilty or ungrateful if you don't show enough appreciation for their efforts.

How to Recognize Them:

- **Overly helpful or unrequested assistance:** The "savior" constantly looks for ways to help, even when it's not needed, imposing themselves as indispensable.

- **Tendency to emphasize their role as the "savior" or "martyr":** They frequently talk about their sacrifices and how much they do for their partner, constantly seeking recognition.

- **Negative reactions when the partner tries to be independent:** When the partner attempts to assert their independence, the "savior" may react with resentment, frustration, or even anger.

- **Use of manipulative phrases:** Phrases like *"Without me, you couldn't make it"* or *"I'm doing this only for* *your own good"* are common to keep the victim in a perceived state of weakness.

Subtle Warning Signs:

- **Difficulty accepting rejection of their help:** They show irritation or frustration if their help is refused or if the partner tries to solve their own problems independently.

- **Creation of dependency situations:** They try to put you in situations where you depend on them, for example by making important decisions for you or controlling aspects of your life.

- **Induced guilt:** They make you feel guilty if you don't accept their help or if you try to become more autonomous, suggesting that you don't appreciate what they do for you.

Motivations: Why Some People Resort to Love Bombing

To fully understand the phenomenon of love bombing, it's not enough to identify who practices it: it's essential to also explore **why**. What are the motivations that drive some people to use love as a weapon, a trap, or a game of power? The reasons can be many, complex, and often intertwined. These individuals don't always act consciously or with premeditation; often, behind their behaviors are deep fears, unmet needs, or unresolved emotional wounds.

Let's explore some of the main motivations that can drive someone to resort to love bombing.

1. Need for Validation and Fragile Self-Esteem

At the core of many love bombers' behavior is a deep and insatiable need for validation. These people may have fragile self-esteem and rely entirely on others' approval to feel important, desirable, or worthy of love. Love bombing thus becomes a way to obtain the emotional gratification they constantly crave. By bombarding the other person with affection and attention, they seek to receive immediate emotional rewards that compensate for their inner sense of emptiness.

Why It Happens:

When self-esteem is based solely on how others perceive us, love becomes a form of emotional "fuel." The feeling of being adored, of having someone dependent on them, or seeing themselves as "perfect" offers the love bomber temporary reassurance about their worth. But this reassurance is short-lived, driving them to constantly seek new ways to feed their fragile ego.

The pursuit of external validation often hides a deeper fragility. Many love bombers may have learned early on that their value is tied to how much they can please or conquer others. Some may have developed an insecure attachment pattern in childhood, where parental love was conditional or unstable. They repeat this pattern as adults, constantly seeking reassurances that are never enough to fill the inner void.

2. Fear of Abandonment and Rejection

Behind love bombing can also lie a deep fear of abandonment. Some people resort to this tactic to prevent the other from leaving, to "seal" the bond as quickly as possible, ensuring that the partner won't abandon them. These individuals may have a history of abandonment or unresolved emotional traumas, which leads them to see every relationship as a potential threat.

Why It Happens:

For them, love bombing is a way to create a rapid and intense attachment, hoping the other becomes dependent on the affection they receive. They think, *"The more I invest now, the harder it will be for them to leave tomorrow."* However, this motivation often has the opposite effect: the relationship becomes suffocating, and the partner may feel trapped, increasing the risk of separation.

The fear of abandonment often has roots in emotional traumas or significant losses experienced in the past. These people may develop a "scarcity mentality" in relationships, where love is perceived as a limited resource that could be taken away at any moment. Investing everything from the start becomes a strategy to prevent any possible separation, but it ends up achieving the opposite result.

3. Need for Control and Power

For some, love bombing is a deliberate strategy to exercise control and power over others. These individuals see relationships as a competition or game where winning means having total control over the partner. They use affection and attention as tools to gain the emotional submission of the other, manipulating their feelings to maintain dominance.

Why It Happens:

Those who resort to this tactic often perceive control as a necessity to feel secure. They may have a deep need for control to compensate for a sense of inner powerlessness or insecurity. They see their partner not as a companion, but as someone to manage, direct, or keep under their control. Love bombing becomes the initial bait to attract and trap the other person, establishing a dynamic where their will is dominant.

The need for control often hides deep insecurities and a sense of powerlessness that the person can't face openly. These individuals may have grown up in environments where power was exercised coercively or abusively, replicating those same dynamics with their partners.

4. Desire for Conquest and Seduction

Some love bombers are motivated purely by the desire for conquest and seduction. These individuals see courting as a challenge, a game where the main objective is to win the attention and desire of the other person. Love bombing is used as an intense seduction technique to quickly pull the partner into a relationship and achieve an emotional "victory."

Why It Happens:

For these individuals, love bombing is a form of self-gratification: it's about proving to themselves and others that they can conquer anyone they desire. Often, once the goal is achieved, they lose interest and move on to the next challenge. This ongoing cycle of seduction and abandonment isn't driven by a genuine interest in the other person but by a need to confirm their power of attraction and charm.

These individuals may have an obsessive need to prove their worth through their ability to attract and seduce others. Each conquest serves as confirmation of their power, and once the excitement fades, they seek a new challenge.

5. Unawareness and Toxic Relationship Models

Not all love bombers act deliberately or consciously. Some people use love bombing because they've never known another way to love. They may have grown up in family or social contexts where love was confused with control, manipulation, or emotional intensity. For them, love bombing is the only relationship model they know, a pattern they repeat without a real understanding of its toxic dynamics.

Why It Happens:
These individuals have never experienced healthy love based on mutual respect and authenticity. They unconsciously repeat the relational patterns they have lived through, believing that love must always be intense, dramatic, or overwhelming. They don't realize that their way of loving is harmful and can cause long-term suffering.

People who learned to equate love with a whirlwind of conflicting emotions and constant drama tend to replicate these patterns in adulthood. This type of love bomber may not necessarily want to harm but has never had models of healthy and reciprocal relationships to learn from.

6. Attraction to Drama and Emotional Instability
Some love bombers are drawn to drama and emotional instability. For them, relationships are a battlefield where emotional intensity is seen as proof of passion or authenticity. Love bombing allows them to create a relationship where emotions are always at their peak, even if that means alternating between

moments of overwhelming affection and periods of conflict and manipulation.

Why It Happens:

These individuals may struggle to manage calmer emotions or more stable relationships. They see stability as monotony and feel more alive in situations of emotional chaos. Love bombing thus becomes a means of constantly fueling this drama, maintaining a relationship that is always intense, even if deeply unstable.

Those attracted to drama might view stability as boring and actively seek conflict to feel alive. They create unstable dynamics to maintain high emotional intensity, confusing turmoil with passion.

Beyond Labels: Recognizing Manipulative Behaviors

The psychological profiles described above represent some of the most common types of people who practice love bombing, but they don't cover every possibility. People are complex, and they often defy rigid classifications that reduce someone to a cliché and obscure the recognition of actual behaviors.

Limiting yourself to identifying someone solely through a psychological label can become a trap for those trying to understand. It's much more useful to focus on concrete behaviors and the dynamics that emerge in the relationship, regardless of the other person's "profile." The important thing to understand is that love bombing is never an act of sincere love but a form of manipulation that can have profound and lasting consequences.

Behavioral Patterns and Warning Signs

Recognizing love bombing in its early stages is essential for protecting yourself from its consequences. Despite the varying motivations, the behaviors of a love bomber follow recurring patterns designed to deeply engage and make the partner dependent and vulnerable.

- **Exaggerated Displays of Affection and Premature Attention**
  One of the first signs of love bombing is an intense and early demonstration of affection. The love bomber tends to flood the other person with attention, gifts, declarations of love, and constant messages. These gestures may seem extraordinary and flattering at first but are often disproportionate to the time spent and the knowledge of each other. Phrases like "I've never loved anyone like I love you" or "You're my soulmate"

spoken after only a few weeks are red flags.

- **Relationship Acceleration: The Need for "All and Now"**

  The love bomber tends to push the relationship forward at an abnormal speed and intensity, talking early about the future, marriage, moving in together, or long-term plans, even when the relationship has just begun. This emotional acceleration is designed to create a rapid attachment, preventing the partner from calmly reflecting on the nature of the relationship. Insistent phrases like "We should live together" or "You're the person I want to spend the rest of my life with" without a solid foundation are warning signs.

- **Emotional and Social Isolation**

  A love bomber seeks to isolate their partner from their support networks, such as friends and family, to make them more dependent. This isolation may start with subtle criticisms or manipulative comments about the partner's friends or family, insinuating that they don't understand the "depth" of your love or that they're "jealous" of the relationship. Comments like "Your friends don't understand how special we are" or "Your family is too critical of us" aim to distance the partner from their loved ones.

- **Alternation Between Intense Attention and Sudden Withdrawal**
  The love bomber alternates moments of overwhelming affection with periods of coldness or withdrawal, creating emotional confusion in the partner. This alternation creates an atmosphere of insecurity, making the manipulated person constantly try to "earn" the affection that was so abundant at the beginning, not realizing that this emotional roller coaster is what makes them vulnerable and dependent.

- **Emotional Manipulation Through Guilt and Fear**
  Emotional manipulation is a cornerstone of love bombing. The love bomber can use guilt or fear to maintain emotional control over their partner. Phrases like "If you leave me, I'll be destroyed" or "I don't understand why you won't do this for me after everything I've done for you" are used to make the other person feel responsible for the love bomber's well-being, forcing them to submit to their demands.

- **Creating Emotional and Psychological Dependency**
  One of the love bomber's main goals is to create emotional and psychological dependency. This is achieved through constant praise and the alternation of criti-

cism, making the partner feel perpetually inadequate or in need of approval. Every time the partner tries to assert their autonomy, the love bomber may react with resentment, causing them to doubt their abilities and independence.

- **Control Through Jealousy and Invasion of Privacy**

  The love bomber may exhibit extreme jealousy, disguised as love or concern. They may want to know where you are, who you're with, and what you're doing at all times, even going as far as checking your phone or messages. These behaviors are often justified as signs of **"protection"** or **"love,"** but in reality, they are tools to monitor and control your every move.

- **Devaluation of Personal Needs and Boundaries**

  The love bomber tends to devalue or ignore their partner's personal needs and boundaries. They may insist on doing things the partner doesn't want, minimizing their concerns or desires, and accusing them of being selfish or ungrateful if they attempt to establish limits. This behavior serves to weaken the other person's ability to say no, making them more vulnerable to further manipulation.

It's not necessary to identify a specific psychological "profile" to recognize manipulative behavior. The most important thing is to pay attention to the signs that emerge in the relationship. If you notice these behaviors repeating, and they seem designed to destabilize, control, or make you feel inadequate, it's time to reflect on the nature of what you're experiencing.

Chapter 4: The Effects of Love Bombing on the Victim

When we talk about love bombing, the focus is often on the person who practices it, but it is equally important to understand what happens to those who experience it. Behind what initially seems like an overwhelming display of affection lies a much more complex and painful reality. The victims of love bombing not only experience intense emotions but also suffer a psychological impact that can leave deep and difficult-to-heal scars.

In this chapter, we will examine how victims transition from initial euphoria to confusion, how anxiety and insecurity slowly creep in, changing their view of themselves and the reality around them. We will analyze how love bombing can erode self-esteem and alter identity, trapping the person in a dynamic that is difficult to escape.

We will discover what happens when love becomes a trap, and how the consequences of this emotional manipulation can profoundly affect the life and well-being of those who experience it.

The Psychological Impact: From Euphoria to Confusion

At first, love bombing seems to offer a unique and overwhelming experience, a love that manifests with intoxicating intensity. It is a period where everything appears extraordinary, almost magical: the victim feels special, adored, as if they have finally found the partner of their dreams. Every word and every gesture from the love bomber seems crafted to create an immediate and total sense of belonging, as if the universe had conspired to unite two soulmates. But just when this euphoria seems to peak, something begins to crack.

The Trap of Happiness: When Euphoria Turns into Dependency

What many victims fail to recognize immediately is that this initial euphoria is a form of induced emotional dependency. The brain, flooded with dopamine—the neurotransmitter associated with reward and pleasure—starts to crave more and more of that "dose" of gratification that comes from the love bomber's affectionate gestures. Every time the partner expresses love or admiration, a reward circuit is activated in the victim's brain, reinforcing the emotional bond.

Dopamine acts as a sort of "emotional glue" that binds the victim to the love bomber. Every compliment, every affectionate gesture, or declaration of love creates a chemical response in the brain that generates a sense of euphoria. But this is not genuine love; it is psychological conditioning. Like a pendulum, the victim swings between moments of extreme happiness and a profound sense of emptiness each time the affection wanes. This is where the trap tightens: the emotional roller coaster becomes a cycle of constant seeking for the same emotional intensity.

The False Promises of Security
In this context, the love bomber may promise eternal love, a connection that seems unique and irreplaceable. But these promises are nothing more than an illusion designed to create a psychological anchor. When the victim starts to perceive the relationship as their main source of security and meaning, they become increasingly vulnerable to manipulation and sudden mood changes.

The Shift from Light to Shadow: When Confusion Creeps In

After the first period of euphoria, the love bomber changes tactics. What was once a constant flow of affection and attention begins to alternate with moments of emotional distance, subtle criticism, and devaluing comments. The victim, who has now tasted the illusion of perfect love, struggles to understand what is happening. They suddenly find themselves walking on unstable ground, where nothing is as clear as before.

Confusion is a subtle but powerful weapon. It prevents the victim from assessing the situation with clarity and making decisions based on concrete facts. In this phase, the manipulated person often finds themselves wondering: "Is it my fault? Did I do something wrong? Why have things changed?" This constant state of uncertainty creates an underlying anxiety that gradually undermines their confidence in themselves and their perception of reality.

The Trap of Justification

Often, the victim starts to justify the love bomber's behavior: "Maybe they're going through a tough time" or "Perhaps they're just stressed." These rationalizations only serve to reinforce the toxic bond, preventing the victim from seeing things for what they truly are: a deliberate attempt to emotionally destabilize them.

Confusion as a Manipulation Tactic: Creating Uncertainty to Maintain Control

Confusion is one of the main tactics used by the love bomber to maintain control. When the victim is trapped in a state of perpetual uncertainty, it becomes much easier to manipulate them. The manipulated person never knows exactly what to expect and, as a result, is less inclined to question the relationship or establish clear boundaries.

Uncertainty creates a state of "emotional alertness." The victim is constantly focused on how to avoid further conflicts or how to regain the lost affection. This continuous effort to predict and prevent negative reactions from the love bomber becomes a form of subtle but effective mental control.

The Paradox of Intermittent Affection

One of the most effective techniques used by love bombers is the alternation between affection and withdrawal. It's like giving and taking away oxygen: the victim becomes dependent on the "breath" of love they are granted intermittently. This intermittent reinforcement is much more powerful than constant affection, as it creates an insatiable desire to recapture the intensity of the early moments. The love bomber can use this technique to gain more and more control over the victim, who feels constantly suspended between hope and despair.

The Descent into Deep Confusion: When Reality Becomes Blurred

As confusion increases, the victim begins to lose their sense of reality. They may feel that they can no longer trust their own perceptions or judgments. Ambiguity becomes the new normal. Situations that would have once been deemed unacceptable are now tolerated or rationalized as part of an "intense" and "complicated" love. This emotional fog is exactly what the love bomber aims to create in order to maintain their psychological grip.

In the long run, this state of chronic confusion can lead to symptoms of post-traumatic stress, generalized anxiety, depression, and a reduced ability to make autonomous decisions. The person feels trapped in a sort of emotional limbo, unable to move in any direction. Often, they begin to depend more and more on the love bomber's opinions and judgments, yielding to every request in an attempt to restore "peace" and regain the initial euphoria.

The Effect of "Cognitive Dissonance": When the Mind Rebels Against Itself

Cognitive dissonance is that strange and uncomfortable sensation you feel when your mind rebels against what your heart is trying to believe. On the one hand, you want to cling to the memory of those magical moments—that overwhelming love that made you feel special like never before. On the other hand, you cannot ignore the pain and confusion that now dominate your reality. This inner struggle is exhausting: you wonder if you're overreacting, if there is indeed a good reason behind the love bomber's behavior.

It's like trying to solve an impossible puzzle: two pieces that don't fit, but you keep trying to push them together, hoping they'll somehow align. And so, to alleviate the discomfort, you begin to justify their actions, telling yourself that all this chaos makes sense, that perhaps this is what real love is—full of highs and lows. But this is just another illusion created by the love bomber to keep you trapped in a cycle of uncertainty and emotional dependency.

Anxiety, Insecurity, and Emotional Dependency

When the initial euphoria of love bombing starts to fade and confusion sets in, victims often experience an escalation of negative emotions that can deeply impact their psychological well-being. Among these, anxiety, insecurity, and emotional dependency become the most evident and devastating symptoms. These feelings do not emerge out of nowhere; they are the result of a constant and calculated process of manipulation designed to destabilize and control.

Anxiety: The Weight of Constant Uncertainty

Anxiety is one of the most common and debilitating psychological effects of love bombing. The emotional roller coaster between affection and coldness, so typical of this dynamic, creates an atmosphere of uncertainty that fuels a constant state of tension. The victim is always on edge, teetering between the desire to please and the fear of losing the approval and affection of the love bomber.

Imagine living each day as if you were walking on eggshells, unsure if the next step will lead to a passionate declaration of love or a cold silence. This uncertainty is exasperating: the victim is constantly in a state of hypervigilance, always searching for signals or clues that might predict the next shift in the love bomber's mood. It's like trying to decipher an indecipherable code, desperately trying to avoid conflict or regain the lost affection.

Anxiety, in this context, is not just emotional discomfort; it becomes a control mechanism. The victim, fearing rejection or abandonment, is forced to behave in increasingly conforming ways to meet the manipulator's desires. Every gesture, every word, every action is calibrated to avoid conflict or disapproval, leading to a constant state of emotional and psychological alertness.

The Cycle of Anxiety in Love Bombing

Anxiety follows a precise cycle within the dynamics of love bombing. Initially, it manifests as mild concern, often masked by the euphoria phase. The victim feels a slight unease, a need for reassurance, a constant desire to keep the level of attention and affection they received from the beginning. This phase is characterized by a continuous search for approval, small signals that everything is fine and that the intensity of love is not diminishing.

When the love bomber starts to withdraw, even slightly, the anxiety increases. In this phase, the victim enters a mode of "hyper-vigilance": every word, every gesture from the love bomber is scrutinized, analyzed, weighed. Every little change becomes a possible signal of an imminent crisis. This growing anxiety is a response to the fear of losing the only source of security and affection they have relied on.

If the love bomber shows signs of irritation or emotionally distances themselves, the anxiety reaches its peak. The victim, now deeply conditioned by the cycle of gratification and deprivation, can feel paralyzed by the fear of saying or doing the wrong thing. This is when the manipulation becomes most powerful: the victim, eager to restore harmony and return to the initial phase of euphoria, becomes willing to do anything to "earn" the partner's love again.

Insecurity: When Self-Esteem Erodes
Alongside anxiety, insecurity slowly creeps into the victim's mind. The love bomber uses a series of tactics to weaken the partner's self-confidence: devaluing comments, subtle criti-

cisms, comparisons with other people, or constantly questioning the victim's decisions and choices. This process of eroding self-esteem is deliberate and methodical. The victim begins to doubt their own judgment, wondering if every decision they make is right, and often starts questioning their own perception of reality.

Insecurity becomes a constant companion, an inner voice whispering: *"You're not good enough," "You're making mistakes," "You don't deserve better."* This sense of inadequacy can paralyze the victim, rendering them incapable of making independent decisions or standing up for their own needs and boundaries. Every attempt to assert themselves is seen as a threat by the love bomber, who reacts with frustration, criticism, or even emotional punishment, further reinforcing the cycle of insecurity.

Devaluation as a Psychological Weapon
For the love bomber, feeding the victim's insecurity is a way to make them more malleable and dependent. A person who doubts themselves will be less likely to oppose, question, or try to escape the relationship. Insecurity, therefore, is not a side effect, but an active tool of control.

Emotional Dependency: When Love Becomes an Invisible Prison
Anxiety and insecurity fuel a third and insidious effect: emotional dependency. The victim, deprived of their inner security

and now confused by conflicting signals, begins to seek not only affection but also approval and reassurance from the love bomber to feel safe. Every positive gesture from the partner becomes a "reward" that seems to confirm the value of the relationship and the love they are receiving, while every negative gesture is interpreted as a punishment to be avoided at all costs.

Emotional Dependency Built Step by Step

This dependency does not develop suddenly but through a gradual process. At the beginning, the love bomber showers the victim with attention and affection, creating a close and seemingly unbreakable bond. However, over time, this affection is dispensed intermittently, creating a cycle of gratification and deprivation that makes the victim increasingly dependent. The relationship becomes a kind of psychological game where the victim constantly tries to "earn" the love they tasted at the beginning.

Emotional dependency makes the victim incapable of imagining life without the partner, even when the relationship becomes toxic and destructive. A kind of "emotional hunger" develops, in which the manipulated person constantly seeks the approval, affection, and security they were promised at the beginning. This hunger becomes so intense that the victim is willing to sacrifice their own happiness, interests, and even dignity to obtain that reassurance.

The Downward Spiral: When Anxiety, Insecurity, and Dependency Intertwine

When anxiety, insecurity, and emotional dependency intertwine, they create a downward spiral that can lead the victim to a state of total psychological submission. The person not only fears losing the partner but begins to believe that without them, they wouldn't be able to survive emotionally. This belief, built on the unstable ground of manipulation and fear, is one of the most dangerous outcomes of love bombing.

The Final Result: An Invisible Prison

This prison has no physical bars but is made of fears, doubts, and insecurities. The victim feels trapped, unable to see a way out, because their sense of identity has been gradually eroded. In this state, even small acts of rebellion or attempts to assert independence are perceived as enormous risks, too frightening to face.

How Love Bombing Undermines Self-Esteem and Identity

Imagine finding yourself in a room full of distorted mirrors, each one reflecting a different image of you. Some make you look larger, others smaller; some make you appear strong, others fragile and broken. And you, standing in the middle, no longer know what your real face looks like. This is exactly what happens to your self-esteem and identity when you are a victim of love bombing.

While the love bomber manipulates your emotions, they also work to gradually erode your inner confidence and your perception of yourself. At first, you feel seen, appreciated, even idealized—but soon this positive image shatters. The partner who once adored you now begins to throw critical glances your way, make devaluing comments, and question your every decision. And so, little by little, the way you see yourself changes, your self-esteem lowers, and your identity starts to blur.

When Words Become Weapons

At first, the love bomber's words seem to wrap you in a warm embrace: *"You're special," "No one has ever loved you like this," "You're safe with me."* But then, almost imperceptibly, this language changes. The words that once made you feel unique begin to carry subtle insinuations: *"You're not as sure of yourself as you thought," "Maybe you should do more for me," "I don't understand why you're not like how I first met you."*

Every negative comment acts as a small crack in your self-esteem. And these cracks widen, transforming your confidence into vulnerability, making you feel less capable, less deserving of respect. You start to doubt yourself, wondering if maybe the problem is you, if perhaps you really should change something to regain the approval that once seemed guaranteed.

The Process of Devaluation: A Slow but Steady Demolition

The love bomber is skilled at creating a process of gradual devaluation. They will never openly tell you: *"You're worthless,"* because that would be too obvious. Instead, they use more insidious techniques: veiled comparisons with other people, criticisms disguised as advice, conditional praise that makes you feel appreciated only when you do exactly what they want. This process doesn't happen suddenly; it is slow, constant, and methodical. And, little by little, you begin to internalize these messages.

You find yourself changing your behavior, your tastes, your opinions to align with what the love bomber seems to desire. You start to question your qualities, wonder if you are really as good as you once thought, and perceive your flaws as insurmountable. Your identity, which once seemed solid and defined, begins to waver.

The Loss of Personal Boundaries: When Identity Becomes Fluid

One of the most insidious effects of love bombing is the progressive loss of personal boundaries. In the initial phase, you may have lowered your defenses, enthusiastically embracing the idea of such an intense and overwhelming love. But as the relationship progresses, you start to feel that your boundaries—what you once considered sacred and untouchable—are being slowly eroded.

You don't immediately notice the change. You start by saying "yes" to small compromises, thinking it's normal in a relationship. But these compromises grow larger, and soon you find yourself doing things you never imagined doing. You might start dressing a certain way to please the partner, avoiding friends they don't like, or changing your daily habits to conform to what the other desires.

This process strips you of your autonomy and makes your identity fluid, unstable. You no longer know who you are without the partner's approval or control. Every decision seems to depend on their reaction. You find yourself wondering: "What would they think if I did this?" "Will they still love me if I behave this way?"

The Construction of a False Identity: When You Stop Being Yourself

At this point, many victims of love bombing begin to build a sort of false identity, an image of themselves that matches the partner's expectations. This false identity is a desperate attempt to maintain the love and approval they received at the beginning. But in doing so, you betray your true nature, suppress your passions, and set aside your authentic needs.

You become a reflection of the other's desires, and this alienates you more and more from your true self. You begin to feel an internal dissonance, as if you're living a life that doesn't really belong to you. This dissonance creates growing discomfort, but, at the same time, a paralyzing fear of losing the only love that was promised to you as "perfect" and "unique."

The Progressive Fragmentation of Identity: When You No Longer Recognize Who You Are

As the relationship progresses, this loss of identity becomes more evident. You no longer recognize your reflections in the "mirrors" distorted by the love bomber. Every attempt to reclaim your true self seems to encounter insurmountable obstacles. Your self-esteem, now compromised, does not allow you to see your worth beyond the relationship.

You feel fragmented, as if parts of yourself have been scattered along the way. This fragmentation of identity leads to a sense of inner emptiness, of loss of meaning. You may feel as though you're playing a role in your own life, not knowing who the real "you" is anymore. And while you find yourself trapped in this cycle of devaluation and dependency, the love bomber maintains control, exploiting every insecurity to keep their power over you.

Reclaiming Your Identity: A Path to Reconstruction

But not all is lost. Even if love bombing has undermined your self-esteem and compromised your identity, awareness of what has happened is the first step toward healing. Recognizing how you were manipulated gives you the opportunity to start rebuilding who you truly are. You can reconnect with your essence, distinguish your authentic needs from others' expectations, and reclaim your inner strength.

In the next chapter, we will explore exactly how to do this: we will talk about emotional defense strategies, how to recognize manipulative dynamics, and, most importantly, how to distinguish between genuine love and love bombing. It's time to take back control of your life and protect yourself from further harm.

Chapter 5: What to Do If You Are a Victim of Love Bombing

Realizing that you are a victim of love bombing can be a devastating revelation. What once seemed like overwhelming and genuine love suddenly reveals itself as an emotional trap, a form of manipulation disguised as affection. But recognizing the reality of the situation is only the first step. The natural question that arises is: what do you do next?

In this chapter, we will explore how to face love bombing with awareness and inner strength. We will discover strategies to protect yourself emotionally, understand when it's time to seek help, and establish clear and respectful boundaries in relationships. We will also talk about the importance of external support — friends, family, and professionals — and how these figures can help you find your way out of a toxic situation and regain your sense of self.

No matter how deep the manipulation may seem, there is always a way out. Let's prepare to learn how to recognize the manipulator's weapons and build a solid and conscious defense against them.

Emotional Self-Defense Strategies

Being a victim of love bombing can leave you disoriented and vulnerable. It is essential not only to recognize what is happening but also to actively take steps to protect yourself. This section offers practical advice on how to behave and respond directly to manipulative tactics while maintaining your integrity and strengthening your emotional self-defense.

1. Respond Calmly and Assertively

When the love bomber floods the relationship with extreme gestures or over-the-top declarations, it's important to stay in control of your reactions. Reacting impulsively or emotionally can fuel their manipulative behavior. Instead, respond by keeping calm, using clear and assertive language to set your expectations and boundaries.

Practical examples:

- **If you're faced with an excess of attention:** *"I ap-*

preciate your concern, but I'd prefer to take things slowly so we can get to know each other better."

- **If you receive love declarations too quickly:** *"I think it's too soon to talk about such deep feelings. I want to be sure that we really know each other."*

- **When you're given an expensive gift too early in the relationship:** *"Your gesture is appreciated, but I'm not comfortable accepting such a big gift at this point."*

- **If they try to monopolize all your time:** *"I need space for my own interests and to see my friends. It's important for me to maintain balance in my life."*

- **When they insist on making long-term plans:** *"It's better to wait and see how our relationship develops before planning the future."*

Why it works:

Responding with calmness and assertiveness shows that you are aware of the dynamics at play and are not willing to be carried away by emotions. You maintain control of the conversation, avoiding being destabilized. This technique allows you to set healthy boundaries from the start and avoid yielding to unwanted pressures.

2. Question Their Words and Actions

One of the tactics love bombers use is ambiguous phrases or manipulative declarations meant to confuse you and make you feel insecure. Don't accept everything they say as absolute truth. Ask direct questions to challenge their words and actions, forcing them to clarify and justify their statements.

Practical examples:

- **If they say:** *"No one will ever love you like I do,"* respond with: *"Why do you think that?"*

- **If they try to make you feel guilty:** *"Why are you trying to make me feel responsible for how you feel?"*

- **When they claim**, *"I know what's best for you,"* **ask:** *"What makes you think you know my needs better than I do?"*

- **If they declare**, *"You're the only person who truly understands me,"* **respond with:** *"How can you say that when we've known each other for so little time?"*

- **When they suggest you're overreacting:** *"Can you explain what you mean by overreacting?"*

Why it works:

Questioning the love bomber's statements forces them to explain themselves and justify their behavior, reducing their power to manipulate your emotions. This approach helps you stay clear-headed and remain connected to your emotional reality.

3. Use the "Defuse" Technique

The love bomber often uses phrases or behaviors designed to provoke an immediate emotional response. One of the most effective techniques for responding is "defusing" — responding in a neutral way that doesn't give them control over your emotional reaction.

Practical examples:

- **When they make a dramatic declaration like:** *"Without you, my life has no meaning,"* you can respond with: *"I understand you feel that way, but everyone is responsible for their own happiness."*

- **If they try to make you feel guilty for not replying to their messages quickly:** *"I appreciate your concern, but I need my time to reflect."*

- **If they say:** *"I can't live without you,"* **respond with:** *"We are all capable of finding happiness within ourselves."*

- **When they create urgency around a decision:** *"I prefer to think about it calmly before making a deci-*

sion."

- **If they complain:** *"Why don't you ever reply to my messages right away?"*: **respond with:** *"I need time to reply when I can and when I feel ready."*

Why it works:
Defusing neutralizes the effect of emotional manipulation, preventing the love bomber from controlling your emotions or making you feel guilty. This approach allows you to maintain your emotional calm and avoid reacting impulsively to provocations.

4. Be Consistent in Your Responses
Consistency is key to defending yourself from love bombing. The love bomber may try to test your boundaries with changing behaviors. Responding consistently, without giving in to their pressures, shows that you are firm in your decisions.

Practical examples:

- **If you've already expressed a boundary, repeat your stance:** *"I've already told you, I'd prefer not to rush the pace of our relationship."*

- **If they try to guilt-trip you into changing your mind:** *"I understand your point of view, but my position remains the same."*

- **When they try to get you to change your plans:** *"I've already made a commitment, and I can't change it at the last minute."*

- **If they insist on meeting your friends and family too soon:** *"I like to take things slowly and introduce important people into my life at the right time."*

- **When they try to manipulate your responses by changing the tone of the conversation:** *"I stand by my opinion, despite how you are presenting the issue."*

Why it works:
Consistency prevents the love bomber from finding weaknesses in your self-defense, showing that they cannot manipulate you by changing tactics. By maintaining your stance, you demonstrate that you are not willing to give in to their control attempts.

5. Don't Fall for Their "Gaslighting" Tactics
Gaslighting is a form of psychological manipulation that tries to make you doubt your perception of reality. When the love bomber tries to make you feel like you're overreacting or imagining things, stand firm in your beliefs.

Practical examples:

- **If they say,** *"You're overreacting, I didn't mean to make* *you feel that way"*: **respond with:** *"This is my perception, and my feelings are valid."*

- **If they try to rewrite history or deny past behavior:** *"I clearly remember what happened, and I won't accept being made to feel like I misunderstood."*

- **When they accuse you of imagining problems that don't exist:** *"My feelings and observations are valid, and I won't be convinced otherwise."*

- **If they say you're taking things too seriously:** *"It's important for me to take things seriously when it comes to my feelings and well-being."*

- **If they minimize their actions by saying:** *"I was just joking,"* you can respond with: *"It wasn't funny to me, so please don't do it again."*

Why it works:
Affirming your perception of reality helps you maintain control of your narrative and reduces the impact of gaslighting. This approach reinforces your confidence in your perceptions and protects you from psychological manipulation.

6. Maintain Your Emotional Independence

The love bomber seeks to make you emotionally dependent on them by exploiting your vulnerability. Resist this tactic by maintaining your emotional independence and not allowing your self-worth to be determined by how you are treated in the relationship.

Practical examples:

- **Remind yourself:** *"I am whole and worthy on my own."*

- **When you feel the need for validation from the partner, replace it with self-affirmation:** *"I am doing my best, and I deserve respect and genuine love."*

- **If you find yourself constantly wondering what they think of you:** *"My choices and my worth don't depend on their approval."*

- **When you feel like you're becoming too dependent on their opinions:** *"I can listen to their ideas, but I decide what's best for me."*

- **If they try to isolate you from others:** *"I need my relationships and my personal space to feel whole."*

Why it works:
Maintaining emotional independence makes you less vulnerable to the love bomber's attempts to manipulate you through emotional control tactics. Recognizing your intrinsic worth

gives you the strength to resist manipulation and make more conscious decisions.

7. Take Time for Yourself

Love bombing can be overwhelming and confusing. It is essential to take time for yourself to reflect, breathe, and reorganize your thoughts. Don't feel obliged to respond immediately or make hasty decisions.

Practical examples:

- **Clearly state:** *"I need some time to think about this situation."*

- **Set time limits in conversations:** *"I can talk about this later; right now is not the right time for me."*

- **If you feel pressured to make an important decision right away:** *"I'd prefer to think it over and discuss it when I feel ready."*

- **When you feel overwhelmed by an intense discussion:** *"I need a moment to gather my thoughts before continuing."*

- **If they try to involve you in activities that make you uncomfortable:** *"I need to think this through before deciding."*

Why it works:
Taking time allows you to regain mental clarity and not succumb to the pressure of the moment. It gives you the space to evaluate things calmly and make conscious decisions, strengthening your emotional self-defense and autonomy.

Techniques for Establishing Healthy Boundaries

Understanding what boundaries are and how to set them is essential to protect yourself from love bombing and other forms of emotional manipulation. Boundaries are the limits that define what is acceptable to you in a relationship and what is not. They represent invisible lines that separate your emotional, physical, and psychological space from others. Establishing boundaries is not only a way to protect yourself but also to assert who you are and what you want from your life and your relationships.

What Are Boundaries?
Boundaries are healthy and necessary barriers that protect your emotional and physical well-being. Imagine having a "personal territory" that you want to preserve: boundaries are the lines that separate this space from that of another person. Setting boundaries means clarifying what you are willing to tolerate,

what you won't accept, and how you want to be treated by others.

Types of Boundaries and How They Apply to Love Bombing

There are different types of boundaries, each of which can be crucial when dealing with love bombing:

Physical Boundaries

Physical boundaries concern your body and personal space. They determine who can approach you, touch you, or enter your space without your consent.

In the context of love bombing: The manipulator might invade your physical space too quickly, trying to establish excessive or constant physical contact. You might feel uncomfortable when the partner tries to hug, kiss, or touch you too soon in the relationship. It's important to clearly assert if you don't feel comfortable with this kind of behavior:

- *"I'm not ready for this level of physical contact; I'd prefer to take more time."*

- *"I like to have my personal space, especially as we're still getting to know each other."*

Emotional Boundaries

Emotional boundaries protect your feelings and emotions.

They involve the ability to express your emotions freely, without feeling judged or guilt-tripped, and to maintain a healthy emotional distance when necessary.

In the context of love bombing: The manipulator might try to leverage your emotions to bond you emotionally or make you feel guilty. They might declare eternal love too soon, pressuring you to reciprocate their declarations. It's crucial to maintain control of your emotions and remember that you have the right to take the time you need to figure out how you feel:

- *"I understand you have strong feelings, but I need more time to understand mine."*

- *"I'm not ready to talk about certain emotions so early."*

Mental Boundaries
Mental boundaries involve your thoughts, opinions, and beliefs. They allow you to have your ideas without feeling forced to change or hide them to please someone else.

In the context of love bombing: The love bomber might try to manipulate your opinions or belittle your thoughts, making you doubt your ideas or convincing you that only their opinions are valid. It's important to assert your right to maintain your beliefs and respect your point of view:

- *"I respect your opinion, but my view on things is differ-*

ent."

- *"I don't agree with what you're saying, but I think it's important to respect each other's viewpoints."*

Time Boundaries

Time boundaries involve how you choose to use your time. They imply the ability to decide how much time to dedicate to a person or activity without feeling pressured.

In the context of love bombing: The love bomber might try to monopolize all your time, preventing you from pursuing your interests or seeing other people. Setting time boundaries means asserting your right to have time for yourself, your friends, family, and personal activities:

- *"I need to have time for myself and my interests."*

- *"I can't see you every day; I need balance between my private life and our relationship."*

Sexual Boundaries

Sexual boundaries protect your comfort and well-being regarding physical intimacy. They define what you are willing to do or not do in your sexual life.

In the context of love bombing: The love bomber might push for sexual intimacy too soon or without respecting your desires. It's essential to set clear limits on what makes you feel comfortable:

- *"I'm not ready for that kind of intimacy."*

- *"I prefer to take things slow, respecting my own timing and desires."*

Financial Boundaries

Financial boundaries concern how you manage your money, belongings, and resources. They involve deciding what to share and with whom.

In the context of love bombing: The manipulator might try to gain access to your financial resources or give you expensive gifts to create a sense of emotional debt. It's important to clarify that you won't accept pressure in this area:

- *"I don't feel comfortable sharing expenses or money at this stage of the relationship."*

- *"I prefer to manage my finances independently."*

Applying Boundaries in the Context of Love Bombing

In love bombing, the manipulator often tries to invade more than one type of boundary simultaneously, creating a sense of being overwhelmed and confused. To protect yourself, it's crucial to:

- **Recognize the signs of boundary invasion**: Notice when you feel pressured or uncomfortable. **Ask yourself:** *"Am I compromising on one of my limits?"*

- **Act quickly to re-establish your limits**: Don't let small violations become the norm. Take back control by saying "no" or clarifying what is unacceptable to you.

- **Stay true to your boundaries, even in the face of pressure**: Don't feel obligated to explain or justify your limits. Your right to set boundaries is fundamental to your emotional and physical health.

Establishing healthy boundaries in a love bombing situation means defending your right to be yourself, to live according to your values, and to be treated with respect. It's not about building impenetrable walls, but about creating barriers that protect you from emotional manipulation. Boundaries allow you to live in harmony with yourself and build relationships based on mutual respect, rather than control and dependency.

The Importance of Support: Friends, Family, and Professionals

Facing the phenomenon of love bombing alone can be extremely difficult. Manipulative dynamics often lead to doubting your perceptions, emotional isolation, and feeling trapped. For this reason, external support becomes crucial. Turning to trusted people like friends, family, or professionals can provide an objective perspective, help you see things more clearly, and offer the strength needed to leave a toxic relationship.

Involving trusted friends and family is a fundamental first step. They are often the first to notice red flags in a relationship, offering an outside perspective and reminding you of who you really are, beyond the manipulations of a love bomber. A strong support network can help keep your reality and self-esteem intact. Sharing doubts and experiences with someone you trust is essential: talking openly about what you're going through can help clarify your thoughts.

We'll dive deeper into the role of support systems and exit strategies in the next chapter. For now, remember that you're not alone: there are people ready to support you and walk with you on the path to a freer, more authentic life.

Chapter 6: When to Decide Whether to Stay or Leave

There comes a moment in every relationship when you need to stop and ask yourself: *"Am I truly experiencing the love I desire?"* When dealing with love bombing, this question becomes even more urgent. Deciding whether to stay or walk away is never easy. It is not a choice made lightly but a decision that requires courage, clarity, and a deep understanding of yourself and your relationship.

In this chapter, we will explore the signs to watch for, the questions you need to ask yourself, and how to assess whether your relationship is truly nurturing or, instead, draining your energy. We will discover how therapy and personal growth can offer new perspectives and tools to help you make the right decision for you. And if you decide it's time to leave, we'll see how to build a safe and strategic plan to exit the relationship, protecting yourself and your future. It's not just about choosing to stay or go but understanding which choice will allow you to live authentically, with love and respect for yourself.

Evaluating the Relationship: Key Questions to Ask Yourself

When you are at the crossroads of a relationship marked by love bombing, it can be difficult to distinguish between what is real and what is manipulation. Emotions are confused, signals are contradictory, and often the line between authentic love and control is blurred. In these moments, the most important thing you can do is stop and reflect. But how? What questions should you ask yourself to truly evaluate the situation you're in?

1. Do I Feel Heard and Understood?
A healthy relationship is based on mutual listening and understanding. Ask yourself if you truly feel heard by your partner. When you express your thoughts, feelings, or concerns, does your partner respond with empathy, or do they minimize, criticize, or ignore them?

If you feel that your emotions are constantly invalidated or ridiculed, it could be a sign that your partner isn't genuinely interested in knowing you deeply but is only trying to control your perception of the relationship.

2. Does This Relationship Make Me Feel Better or Worse About Myself?

Every relationship should contribute to your well-being, not undermine it. Ask yourself if, since you started this relationship, you feel better about yourself or, conversely, if your self-esteem has plummeted. Do you constantly feel pressured to be someone different from who you are? Do you feel like you constantly need to prove your worth? If the answer is yes, it might be time to seriously consider whether this relationship is positive for you.

3. Am I Free to Be Myself?

A clear sign of a toxic relationship is the feeling that you always have to walk on eggshells or hide parts of yourself to be accepted. Ask yourself if you feel free to be yourself, with all your imperfections, or if you sense a constant judgment that pushes you to change your behavior, your interests, or your friendships to meet your partner's expectations. In a healthy relationship, you should never feel forced to change who you are to receive love or approval.

4. Do I Have Spaces for Autonomy and Independence?

Love bombing often manifests as a constant invasion of your time and personal space. Reflect on your independence: do you feel free to make decisions for yourself, pursue your interests, spend time with your friends and family, or do you feel constantly monitored and controlled? If your partner tries to limit your autonomy, monopolize your time, or make you feel guilty for your choices, it may be a dynamic of control disguised as "attention" and "love."

5. Do I Feel Guilty for Being Happy Without Him/Her?

One of the most common tactics of love bombers is to make you feel guilty for your independence or for moments of happiness that don't involve them. Ask yourself if you feel that your happiness depends exclusively on your partner's presence or approval. If you notice that you feel guilty for experiencing joy outside the relationship, you may be experiencing emotional manipulation aimed at making you emotionally dependent.

6. Does This Relationship Promote Growth or Stagnation?

Authentic love should encourage mutual growth. Ask yourself if this relationship is helping you grow as a person, develop new interests, and explore new parts of yourself, or if you instead feel more limited, stuck, or trapped. If you sense that the relationship is hindering your personal development or making you feel stagnant, it may be time to consider a change.

7. Do I Feel Emotionally Safe and Protected?

Emotional security is the foundation of any healthy relationship. Ask yourself if you feel safe, supported, and emotionally protected. Do you feel you can open up without fear of judgment, retaliation, or manipulation? Or do you sense a constant threat of emotional blackmail, punishment, or sudden distancing? A lack of emotional security is a strong signal that the relationship may not be healthy for you.

8. Am I Compromising My Values?

A healthy relationship should respect and honor your core values. Ask yourself if, in trying to maintain the relationship, you're accepting behaviors you wouldn't normally tolerate. Do you feel forced to do things that don't reflect who you are or to stay silent to avoid conflict? You might notice that you're starting to change your personality or downplay what's important to you. Compromising on what truly matters can be a sign that you're sacrificing too much to maintain a relationship that doesn't respect you.

9. Would I Feel Lost Without This Relationship?

Feeling lost without a relationship is often a sign that emotional dependence has taken over. Ask yourself if your happiness and self-esteem depend solely on your partner's presence. Reflect on how much you have neglected friendships, hobbies, or personal goals to accommodate your partner's desires. If you feel completely lost without this relationship, it may be the result of manipulation that has eroded your independence and sense of self.

10. What Do I Really Want?

Ultimately, everything boils down to this fundamental question: what do you truly want? Beyond fears, confusion, and expectations, what would make you feel truly at peace with yourself? Imagine your ideal life, with or without this relationship. Try to listen to your gut: is there an inner voice guiding you in a specific direction? Reconnecting with this part of yourself will help you make the best decision for you, one that honors your deepest desires and real needs.

Listening to Your Answers

Answering these questions honestly requires courage and self-awareness. Each answer will bring you closer to the truth of your situation and help you decide whether it's worth continuing to invest in this relationship or if it's time to walk away. Remember, your well-being, your emotional security, and your happiness are the priority. Don't be afraid to choose what's best for you.

But making a decision doesn't mean you have to face everything on your own. In the next section, we will explore how therapy and personal growth can offer the support and tools you need to approach this choice with greater awareness and serenity.

The Role of Therapy and Personal Growth

Deciding whether to stay or leave a relationship marked by love bombing is just the first step in a longer journey toward self-awareness and inner growth. Therapy and personal growth can become fundamental tools to help you better understand yourself, your vulnerabilities, and the reasons that may have led you to this situation. Approaching these dynamics with an open and curious mindset allows you to avoid future toxic patterns and build healthier, more fulfilling relationships.

A qualified therapist can help you explore the behavioral patterns that may have made you susceptible to becoming a victim of love bombing, recognize the warning signs in future relationships, and establish healthier personal boundaries. Through therapy, you can learn how to build authentic and mutually satisfying relationships based on trust and mutual respect, rather than manipulation and control.

Additionally, personal growth can offer practical tools to increase your self-esteem, improve your communication skills, and develop greater self-awareness. This path may include reading books on the topic, participating in support groups, or exploring self-reflection practices such as meditation or journaling. The healing process is unique for each person, and finding what works best for you can make a significant difference in your emotional recovery.

Why Were You a Victim of Love Bombing? A Coincidence or Something More?

Being a victim of love bombing can lead to many questions: "Why me?" "What made me vulnerable to this type of manipulation?" While it may seem like an isolated incident, the truth is that there's often a deeper reason behind this experience. It's not about blaming yourself, but about exploring with kindness and curiosity the personal factors that may have predisposed you to fall into this emotional trap.

Some possible factors include:

1. History of Difficult Relationships
If you've had past relationships with manipulative or narcissistic partners, you may have developed, even unconsciously, a higher tolerance for toxic behaviors. Perhaps you've learned to endure or minimize the red flags, finding yourself justifying unacceptable behaviors simply because they seem familiar. Imagine a frog slowly adjusting to water that's gradually heating up: the change is so gradual that, before it knows it, it's in a dangerous and damaging situation. Similarly, in a relationship, you may gradually become trapped in a controlling dynamic without even realizing it.

2. Need for Approval

Growing up in an environment where approval was rare or conditional can create a deep emotional hunger, a desperate desire to be accepted and loved at all costs. This need becomes a dangerous vulnerability in the hands of a love bomber, who knows exactly how to create the illusion of total and unconditional approval, only to suddenly withdraw it, leaving you in a state of dependency. Imagine being like a child who waits in vain for a parent's approval, desperately seeking that "good job!" that always seems out of reach.

3. Fragile Self-Esteem

Low self-esteem can make you more willing to accept any kind of affection, even if it comes from a toxic source. When you don't believe you deserve healthy, genuine love, you may settle for the emotional scraps the love bomber throws your way. It's as if you're trying to fill a void with whatever attention you can get, even if it's sporadic or even negative. You might start thinking that even a little emotional poison is better than nothing, and that a damaged love is the only option available to you.

4. Desire to "Save" the Partner

Some people are naturally drawn to problematic partners, seeing them as "projects" to be saved. This tendency to want to "fix" or "heal" the other with your love can lead to a spiral of mutual dependency. You find yourself investing time and energy trying to repair a sinking ship, only to realize too late that, while trying to save it, you're sinking along with it. This dynamic can make you feel noble, but it's often a form of self-gratification disguised as altruism, which inevitably leads to emotional exhaustion and disappointment.

5. Lack of Clear Boundaries

As discussed in the previous chapter, the absence of clear boundaries can be one of the main reasons you become vulnerable to love bombing. If you find setting boundaries challenging, you may want to revisit that section and reflect on what we explored together. Reviewing those concepts can help you recognize areas of your life where boundaries can be strengthened and protected, preventing relational dynamics that put your emotional well-being at risk.

6. Fear of Loneliness

For many people, the fear of being alone can become a determining factor in staying in dysfunctional relationships. This fear may drive you to ignore obvious signs of manipulation or tolerate harmful behaviors just to avoid the sense of emptiness that isolation can bring. It's like being on an unstable boat in the middle of a storm: even though the boat is leaking, the thought of abandoning it and swimming alone in the open sea seems even more terrifying. So, you stay on board, hoping things will improve, without realizing that you're only sinking deeper.

7. Need for External Validation

When your self-esteem largely depends on the opinions of others, you become particularly susceptible to the initial flattery of the love bomber. You seek external validation because it seems like your worth depends on others' approval, and a love bomber knows how to exploit this dynamic, making you feel special only to destabilize you by suddenly withdrawing that affection. It's like building a house on sand: it seems solid until the tide rises, and it begins to crumble.

8. Tendency to Idealize Love

If you have an idealized vision of love, you may be inclined to believe that relationships should be intense and overwhelming. This can lead you to interpret the exaggerated gestures and grand declarations of the love bomber as signs of true love, when in reality they may hide manipulation and control. Believing that "true love requires sacrifice" can make you ignore your needs and personal boundaries, trapping you in dynamics that are not truly healthy.

These aspects are just some of the reasons that may have made you vulnerable to love bombing. They are not fixed definitions but insights that can help you better understand yourself and make more conscious choices in your future relationships.

How to Build a Plan to Leave the Relationship Safely

Deciding to leave a relationship marked by love bombing can feel like one of the hardest decisions of your life. It's a complex process that requires courage, awareness, and, most importantly, preparation. You may feel a mix of fear, anxiety, and uncertainty, but also a spark of hope, a hope that pushes you to seek a future that's freer, more authentic, and free from the toxic dynamics that have trapped you. In this chapter, we want to guide you through each step of this journey, helping you build a plan that allows you to exit the relationship safely and mindfully.

Prepare Emotionally: Accept the Complexity of Your Choice

The decision to leave a manipulative relationship is rarely clear and simple. It may feel like your heart and mind are in a never-ending battle, with one part of you wanting to stay and another knowing it's time to go. It's important, however, to recognize and accept this complexity. Allow yourself to feel every emotion that comes up: the fear of change, the pain of loss, but also the strength growing within you as you imagine a different future. It's not weakness to feel confused or scared; it's natural when facing a life-altering choice.

Choosing to leave doesn't mean denying what was, but embracing what could be. Imagine your life without that emotional burden, without that constant uncertainty, and see what emerges: the desire to feel light, the possibility of rediscovering yourself, and the ability to reopen your heart to true love. Remember that every emotion you feel, from pain to hope, is part of the healing process.

Create a Support Circle: You're Not Alone on This Journey

As you prepare your exit plan, remember that you don't have to face everything alone. Surround yourself with trusted people who can offer empathetic listening and concrete support. Friends, family, or even a therapist can help you see the situation more clearly and remind you that you deserve much more than manipulative love.

Share your thoughts and decision with these people. Explain to them what you're going through and how they can help. Sometimes, just knowing that someone is on your side can make the difference between feeling trapped and feeling strong enough to take the first step toward freedom. You might also consider joining support groups, where others have had similar experiences; this will give you a sense of belonging and help you understand that you're not alone.

Plan Carefully: Every Detail Counts

Leaving a toxic relationship requires not only courage but also careful planning. Take the time to think through every practical detail that might arise during the process of leaving. Where will you go? What will you need? How will you handle any legal or financial complications? Every little detail matters when it comes to your safety and well-being.

Find a safe place to stay, even if it's just temporary. This could be at a trusted friend's house, a family member's home, or a safe shelter if necessary. Prepare a bag with essential items: documents, money, keys, clothes, and important personal belongings. If you have a pet, consider their needs as well. If necessary, contact a lawyer to better understand your rights and options, especially if shared assets or legal matters are involved.

Also, think about your financial safety: open a separate bank account if possible and set aside some money to support yourself in the initial period after the breakup. This may seem excessive, but it's a precaution that will give you greater autonomy and freedom of choice.

Communicate Your Decision with Clarity and Calm

When the time comes to communicate to your partner that you're leaving, choose a safe time and place. It could be in a public setting, where you're protected by the presence of other people, or with someone you trust nearby, especially if you fear an unpredictable or violent reaction. Clarity is key: be direct but calm. Avoid getting into conflicts or being drawn into endless discussions. Your decision is not up for debate; it's a choice you've made to protect yourself.

Say what you feel with sincerity and firmness: "I can no longer stay in this relationship. This is my decision, and I respect it." Expect various reactions: anger, pleading, promises of change, or even emotional manipulation attempts. Stand firm in your choice, knowing that you are doing what's best for you. Remember, your goal is to protect yourself, and you don't need to justify your decision more than once.

Protect Your Safety: Be Prepared for Any Outcome
Leaving a toxic relationship can sometimes trigger unpredictable reactions. Make sure you have an emergency plan. Share your decision with someone you trust who can intervene if needed. Keep a list of emergency contacts handy, such as friends, family, or even law enforcement if necessary. Never underestimate the risk: if you feel your safety may be compromised, take all necessary precautions.

Consider limiting contact with your partner after the breakup. This may mean blocking phone numbers, cutting off social media connections, and only communicating about essential matters, such as dividing property. This isn't a drastic step but a way to protect your peace and create space for your healing.

Rebuild Your Life with Patience and Dedication

Leaving a manipulative relationship isn't just about escaping; it's the start of a new chapter. Dedicate time to yourself to heal, reconnect with who you truly are, and rediscover what makes you happy. There's no rush, no pressure: this is your time to breathe and rebuild.

Make space for your passions, cultivate new friendships, and reestablish connections with those who may have drifted apart during the relationship. Continue to work on yourself through therapy, meditation, reading, or any form of personal growth that makes you feel connected to yourself. See this period as an opportunity to rediscover what you love and to reconnect with your core values.

Have you ever longed to feel truly safe in your relationships, free to be yourself without fear or compromise?
In the next chapter, we'll explore practical strategies to protect yourself from the dynamics that have hurt you, helping you rediscover your inner strength and feel more secure in your worth. It will be a journey toward healthier and more authentic relationships, where you can finally feel free to be yourself, without the fear of losing who you truly are.

Chapter 7: Building Healthy and Authentic Relationships

After experiencing love bombing, it may seem difficult to imagine a future where you can trust again, where you can open yourself up to new relationships without the fear of being hurt or manipulated. Yet, it is possible. Rebuilding healthy and authentic relationships begins with restoring trust in yourself and in others. This chapter focuses on how to overcome the wounds of the past, build connections based on mutual respect, and develop effective and mindful communication practices.

Because it's not enough to simply understand what to avoid — it's also essential to know what to seek. In these pages, we will explore the steps necessary to create genuine bonds where you feel safe, valued, and free to be yourself. A healthy relationship is not without challenges, but it is a union between two people who support each other, grounded in trust, respect, and authentic love.

Rebuilding Trust in Yourself and Others

Regaining trust after experiencing love bombing is like repairing a torn fabric: it requires time, care, and patience. When someone has manipulated your feelings, your view of the world can become distorted, leaving you doubting your intuition and judgment. Trusting yourself and others may seem like a distant goal, but it is possible to embark on a path toward rebuilding trust through small yet significant steps.

Recognize Your Intrinsic Value

The first step in recovery is recognizing your worth, independent of what others think. After emotional manipulation, it's easy to fall into the trap of measuring your value through the eyes of others. However, separating your self-esteem from external opinions is a liberating act. This is not an immediate change but a gradual process of rediscovering your authenticity.

Cultivating a positive internal dialogue is essential. Each day, take a moment to identify a quality you appreciate about yourself and write it down in a journal, along with concrete examples of how you've expressed it. This exercise helps reinforce your self-perception, based on who you truly are.

Additionally, devote time to activities that make you feel good and give you a sense of accomplishment. Reading, writing, exercising, or simply spending time in nature can help you reconnect with your authentic self, strengthening your self-esteem.

Explore Who You Truly Are

Take time to reflect on who you are, beyond the past relationship. Ask yourself questions like, *"What are my strengths?" "What values are important to me?" "In what situations do I feel my best?"* These reflections can offer new perspectives on yourself, free from external influences. Write down your answers and review them periodically to see how they evolve over time. You may discover new dimensions of yourself that you had never considered before.

You can delve further into this process by asking yourself, *"What makes me unique?" "What experiences have shaped me as a person?" "What do I truly desire in my life, beyond the expectations of others?"* These reflections can be powerful tools for personal growth, helping you build a self-narrative that is true to your real nature.

Create a New Narrative About Yourself

Writing down your reflections is just the beginning. Use these discoveries to create a new narrative about yourself that honors your experiences and intrinsic qualities. This new story should include not only who you are but also who you want to become. Be kind to yourself during this process: it's normal to feel fragile when trying to heal from painful experiences. However, each reflection is another brick in the reconstruction of a stronger, more positive self-image.

Metaphor Example: Imagine your identity as a plant that has been uprooted and placed in the wrong soil, with little light and nourishment. Now, you're transplanting that plant into new soil, a place chosen with care, where it can finally thrive. At first, the leaves may wilt, but with care and attention, the plant will regain its vitality and grow stronger than ever.

Learning to Trust Your Judgment

Love bombing leaves deep scars, changing how we perceive ourselves and the world around us. One of its most insidious effects is eroding trust in your own judgment. After a manipulative experience, it can be difficult to distinguish between what you truly feel and what has been influenced by others. Learning to trust your instincts again takes time and practice.

Developing a trusting relationship with yourself doesn't mean ignoring others' opinions, but rather learning to evaluate those opinions in light of your own perceptions. Your emotions and thoughts have value and deserve attention. When facing a decision or ambiguous situation, ask yourself, *"What do I really feel?" "What are the facts, and what are my personal interpretations?"* This mindful reflection allows you to separate what is real from what is influenced by fears or past experiences.

Self-Validation Exercise: Each time you face a decision, big or small, pause for a moment and ask yourself: *"How does this decision make me feel?" "What are the options, and what are the consequences of each?"* Write down your responses, paying attention to how your body reacts. If a choice causes anxiety or distress, explore why. Often, the answer is hidden in the folds of your unexpressed thoughts and feelings.

Practicing self-validation regularly helps you recognize and respect your instincts, distinguishing between irrational fear and authentic intuition. Over time, you'll start to notice that your perceptions are often accurate and valid, even when faced with conflicting opinions. This strengthens a solid foundation of trust in yourself.

Giving Yourself Permission to Make Mistakes

Learning to trust yourself doesn't mean never making mistakes. Mistakes are part of the learning and growth process. Each time you make an error, instead of harshly judging yourself, ask: *"What can I learn from this experience?"* Every misstep is an opportunity to better understand yourself and your limits. Give yourself permission to make mistakes and grow through these experiences, knowing that self-trust is an ongoing journey, not a final destination.

Metaphor Example: Trusting your judgment is like learning to navigate a boat. At first, you may feel unsure of how to handle the waves and currents. But the more you trust your ability to read the sea and adapt, the smoother the navigation becomes. There may be stormy moments, but with each challenge, you gain skill and confidence, learning to guide your boat with trust, knowing you're capable of facing any sea.

Cultivating Patience: Trust Is Not Rebuilt in a Day

Rebuilding trust, once broken, takes time. It is not a linear process, nor something that can be rushed. It is like a flower that needs time to develop strong roots before it can bloom again. Every small step, no matter how insignificant it may seem, is a testament to growth and resilience.

There will be days when everything seems to go wrong, moments when insecurity or doubt resurface. In these instances, it's easy to view each misstep as a failure, but in reality, these moments are an integral part of the healing journey. Every stumble offers the opportunity to learn, better understand your emotions, and develop new strategies for facing future difficulties.

When you encounter these moments of uncertainty, give yourself the right to feel vulnerable without judging yourself. Ask, *"What are the reasons behind my emotions?"* Perhaps old wounds are reopening, or new fears are emerging. These moments of reflection can become valuable opportunities to better understand what is troubling you and find ways to deal with it more mindfully.

Gradually Opening Up to Others

After a painful experience, the prospect of trusting again can seem daunting. The fear of being hurt may lead you to close yourself off, but total isolation is not the solution. Starting with small gestures can help you regain trust in others.

Attending protective and welcoming environments, joining interest groups, or participating in volunteer activities can be a good starting point for approaching others without feeling pressured. Observe how people respond to your thoughts and emotions. Signs like attentive listening, empathetic responses, or acts of kindness are valuable indicators to understand who is open to building an authentic connection with you.

Carefully evaluate the quality of the relationships you choose to build, seeking people who respect your boundaries and are willing to share moments of mutual support. Maintaining an open yet cautious attitude will help you avoid falling back into toxic dynamics and recognize those who genuinely care about your well-being.

Strengthen Bonds with Those Who Have Proven to Be Trustworthy

After experiencing love bombing, it's easy to think that all relationships follow the same manipulative pattern. However, not all connections from the past were harmful. Some people, even during the toughest times, have shown themselves to be reliable, respecting your boundaries and offering genuine support.

These relationships are tangible proof that respect and empathy do exist. Use them as an antidote to the doubt instilled by love bombing. When you find yourself thinking that every bond is potentially manipulative, remember these relationships that made you feel safe.

Invest time and attention in strengthening these bonds: plan regular meet-ups, engage in common activities, or simply maintain constant communication. Every shared moment can serve to strengthen your sense of security and remind you that there are trustworthy people.

Accept That Complete Trust May Not Always Be Possible, and That's Okay

When you've gone through love bombing, it's normal to feel torn between the desire to protect yourself and the urge to trust again. Love bombing, with its load of manipulations and false promises, can leave you feeling wary and unsure about who is truly deserving of your trust. But here's a truth that may relieve you: you don't have to blindly trust everyone to prove that you've healed.

Trust is a personal choice, not an obligation. There's no need to adhere to a universal model of trust; every healing journey is unique. Acknowledge that trust isn't a goal but a journey that evolves with your experiences. Celebrate each step toward trust as a sign of inner strength without forcing anything. Every time you choose to trust, do it on your own terms, at your own pace. That is more than enough.

Creating Connections Based on Mutual Respect

When we talk about mutual respect in a relationship, the focus is often on what not to do: don't be overbearing, don't control, don't manipulate. But what does it really mean to build a connection founded on genuine and deep respect? It's more than just avoiding certain behaviors; it's an active commitment to valuing the other person, creating a balance between giving and receiving, and supporting each other at every moment.

Prioritizing the Freedom to Be Yourself

A connection based on respect begins when both people feel free to be who they are, without the pressure to change in order to meet the other's expectations or desires. This means accepting your partner in their uniqueness, with all their flaws and virtues, without trying to mold them into your own image. Freedom isn't synonymous with distance, but rather a deep sense of security in being able to express your individuality.

Think about relationships where you truly felt free to be yourself: what made them different? It was likely the feeling of being heard without judgment, sensing that the other person respected your timing, your space, and your needs. Creating this kind of space in a relationship requires active listening and a willingness to set aside your own ego in order to truly see the other person.

Clearly Expressing Your Needs and Desires

Mutual respect is also built through honest and direct communication. In many relationships, misunderstandings arise because one or both partners are afraid to say what they really think or want. They fear seeming selfish, hurting the other, or disrupting a fragile balance. But hiding your needs only leads to resentment and frustration.

To build a strong and healthy bond, it's essential to speak openly about what you want, without manipulating or imposing your will. Expressing a need or desire doesn't mean asking for the impossible — it's an invitation to create common ground where both partners can feel satisfied and respected.

Recognizing the Value of Active Listening

Active listening goes beyond just hearing what the other person is saying — it means genuinely engaging with their words, emotions, and the context from which they are speaking. This requires attention, an open mind, and sometimes the willingness to question your own beliefs. When you practice active listening, you show the other person that you value their voice, that their thoughts and feelings matter.

For example, instead of interrupting or immediately responding, take a moment to reflect on what has been said and, if needed, ask for clarification: *"I'd like to understand better what you mean"* or *"How did you feel in that situation?"* This simple act can profoundly transform the quality of the connection.

Supporting the Other's Autonomy

In a relationship based on respect, each partner recognizes and supports the other's autonomy. This means encouraging your partner to follow their own dreams, pursue their passions, and make their own decisions, even when these don't perfectly align with your expectations.

Autonomy should never be seen as a threat but as a sign of a healthy relationship. Accepting that the other person has a life, interests, and projects outside the relationship is crucial to building a genuine connection. This not only strengthens mutual trust but also fosters a sense of balance and equality.

Practicing Unconditional Acceptance

Unconditional acceptance is the ability to love and respect the other person for who they are, without trying to change them to fit your expectations. In a respectful relationship, both partners feel accepted without conditions or compromises. This doesn't mean ignoring flaws or tolerating unacceptable behavior but rather seeing the other as a whole, deserving of love and respect just as they are.

When you practice unconditional acceptance, you show the other that they don't have to be perfect to deserve love. You're saying, *"I see who you really are, and I like what I see."* This attitude creates an environment where the other feels safe being themselves without fear of judgment or rejection.

Committing to Growing Together, Not Apart

Finally, mutual respect manifests in the willingness to grow together as a couple. This means facing challenges as a team, seeking to understand the lessons that each experience brings, and finding ways to support each other in times of change or crisis. A respectful relationship is dynamic, adapting and evolving with the needs of both partners.

Investing in mutual growth involves recognizing that neither partner has all the answers but that both have much to learn. It also means being willing to question your own beliefs and face your own limitations, not to change the other but to build a connection that is flexible and resilient.

8 Steps for Authentic and Effective Communication

Communicating clearly and mindfully is crucial for building healthy relationships. After experiencing love bombing, you may feel insecure about sharing your thoughts and feelings, fearing that you'll be misunderstood or manipulated. However, only through authentic communication can you create deep and meaningful connections. Here are some key strategies to improve your communication and foster genuine connections:

1. Be Clear and Direct

Clarity prevents misunderstandings and strengthens trust. Express what you think and feel directly, avoiding ambiguity or hidden meanings. Don't expect the other person to read between the lines: if you have a need, state it clearly, such as "I need more time for myself" or *"I'd like you to listen without interrupting."* Clear communication creates a sincere connection and reduces the risk of misunderstandings.

Being direct doesn't mean being harsh. Use language that respects the other person's emotions, starting with phrases like *"I feel"* or *"I need."* This not only clarifies your point of view but makes it easier for the other person to respond empathetically.

2. Listen Attentively

Effective listening goes beyond simply hearing — it requires active presence and genuine interest in what the other person is saying. Avoid thinking about your response while the other is speaking; instead, focus entirely on them. Practice active listening by repeating what you've understood, such as *"If I understood correctly, you feel that..."* This technique shows that you are committed to the conversation and eager to truly understand the other person.

Active listening not only facilitates mutual understanding but also builds an atmosphere of openness and trust, essential for any deep dialogue.

3. Use "I" Statements Instead of "You" Statements

When communicating your feelings or needs, use phrases that start with *"I" instead of "You."* Saying *"I feel neglected when this happens..."* is much more effective than *"You never pay attention to me,"* as it avoids directly accusing the other person and reduces the likelihood of defensiveness.

"I" statements help you express your emotions honestly without making the other person feel attacked, fostering open and constructive dialogue.

4. Be Receptive to Feedback and Accept Constructive Criticism

Being open to feedback, even when it's uncomfortable, is essential for mindful communication. Consider criticism as an opportunity for growth, not a personal attack. When you receive criticism, remain calm and show openness by responding with statements like, *"I understand your point of view, can you explain more?"* or *"Thank you for sharing this with me, I'll think about it."*

This approach encourages dialogue and strengthens the bond, creating an environment of mutual learning.

5. Express Emotions Authentically

Don't be afraid to show what you truly feel. Expressing emotions, even difficult ones, is essential for building genuine connections. Avoiding discussions about your feelings can prevent true intimacy.

Clearly state how you feel: *"I feel frustrated when this happens"* or *"I'm happy when we do this together."* Expressing emotions authentically creates a space for sharing and understanding, where both of you can feel safe to be yourselves.

6. Avoid Power Struggles

Discussions shouldn't be competitions to prove who is right but opportunities to better understand each other. If you notice that you're trying to "win" a conversation, pause and ask yourself, *"Am I trying to understand or to prevail?"* Effective communication isn't about control but about finding solutions that work for both.

A respectful and open dialogue promotes trust and intimacy, steering clear of power struggles.

7. Ask Open-Ended Questions

To encourage deeper dialogue, ask questions that prompt the other person to fully express themselves, like *"What do you think about this situation?"* or *"How did you feel about what happened?"* Open-ended questions encourage genuine reflection and help both partners explore their feelings more thoroughly. These questions demonstrate a genuine interest and foster more meaningful communication.

8. Practice Awareness of Non-Verbal Communication

Body language, tone of voice, and eye contact are fundamental in communication. An open posture, a genuine smile, and a calm tone of voice can convey empathy and openness. Similarly, pay attention to the other person's non-verbal signals to better understand their emotions.

Being aware of non-verbal communication reinforces the message you want to convey and helps create an atmosphere of trust and mutual respect.

By integrating these communication practices, you lay the foundation for healthier, more respectful, and authentic relationships.

Conclusion

You've done something extraordinary. You've reached the end of this journey and faced uncomfortable truths, looking within yourself and recognizing that you deserve more. You've chosen to learn how to build a different future, one where love is authentic, respectful, and mutual. It hasn't been easy, but the fact that you've made it this far demonstrates your strength and determination.

Together, we've walked through the maze of love bombing, uncovering how, behind those seemingly sweet and overwhelming gestures, lies one of the most insidious forms of manipulation. We've explored the origins of this phenomenon, why some people engage in it, and how deeply it can hurt those who fall victim to it. We've delved into its emotional and psychological effects.

But you didn't stop there. You've learned to distinguish between real love and manipulation, to recognize the warning signs, and to understand the dynamics of these toxic relationships. Admitting that you've been a victim of love bombing is difficult, but you've already taken the biggest step: you've acknowledged it. This is the starting point for change.

Taking control of your life isn't easy, but together, we've explored practical tools to protect yourself emotionally, establish healthy boundaries, and deal with toxic people with calmness. Most importantly, you've discovered how to rebuild trust in yourself and others. Yes, it's a process that takes time, but now you know it's possible.

Now, you're ready for the future. You've faced the dilemma of whether to stay or leave, and you've learned to ask yourself the right questions to determine whether a relationship is healthy. We've discussed the importance of therapy, personal growth, and how to plan a safe way out, if necessary. You're now prepared to build relationships based on mutual respect, open communication, and shared growth.

But this is only the beginning. Real change happens when you put into practice what you've learned. Imagine your life as a book, and now you hold the pen. Up until today, some pages may have been written by others, but from now on, you will decide the plot, who to include in your journey, and which chapters will define who you truly are and what you desire.

Healing from love bombing and building healthier relationships requires time, patience, and a lot of self-love. There will be moments when you may want to turn back, but each time you choose to pause and reflect, you are rewriting your story — a story of strength, resilience, and true love.

Building a support network will be essential on this journey. Surround yourself with people who love and respect you for who you are, without conditions. Friends, family, and professionals can be valuable resources in difficult times, helping you stay grounded during challenging moments and discover new possibilities when you're ready.

Now you have the tools to make intentional choices. It's no longer about the fear of being alone or accepting anything just to have company. Now, you know that you can invest only in relationships that help you grow, respect you, and value you. Every mindful choice you make will be a step toward a more authentic and fulfilling life.

Before we conclude, it's important to debunk some of the most common myths about love bombing. These myths prevent us from recognizing manipulation for what it truly is. Understanding the truth behind them will help you distinguish more clearly between genuine love and manipulative behavior. Here are the 15 most common myths related to love bombing and the truths that debunk them:

15 Myths & Truths About Love Bombing

1. **Myth:** Love bombing is just a demonstration of intense love.
   Truth: Love bombing is emotional manipulation, designed to create dependence and control.

2. **Myth:** It only happens in romantic relationships.
   Truth: Friendships, family, or work relationships can also exhibit love bombing dynamics.

3. **Myth:** If someone showers you with attention, it's because they truly love you.
   Truth: Excessive and disproportionate attention is often a sign of manipulation.

4. **Myth:** Love bombing only appears at the beginning of a relationship.
   Truth: It can also surface later on to regain control of the relationship.

5. **Myth:** Strong people don't fall victim to love bombing.

Truth: Love bombing can affect anyone, as it exploits vulnerabilities often unseen.

6. **Myth:** If you have doubts about the relationship, it means you're not in love.
Truth: Doubts are normal, especially in the presence of manipulative dynamics.

7. **Myth:** The love bomber acts unconsciously.
Truth: Many love bombers are fully aware of their manipulation and use it as a tool of power.

8. **Myth:** Leaving a love bombing relationship is easy once you become aware of it.
Truth: Leaving a love bombing relationship requires strength and planning, as emotional dependence can be deep.

9. **Myth:** All intense relationships are love bombing.
Truth: Intensity isn't the problem; the attempt to control and manipulate is what defines love bombing.

10. **Myth:** The love bomber truly loves you, even if they express their love in the wrong ways.
Truth: Love bombing isn't love, but a tactic of emotional control.

11. **Myth:** Love bombing always leads to physical vio-

lence.

Truth: Not all manipulative relationships become physically violent, but emotional manipulation is already a form of abuse.

12. **Myth:** Confronting the love bomber will make them change.
    Truth: Many love bombers don't change, even if they promise to.

13. **Myth:** Accepting love bombing means being weak.
    Truth: Anyone can fall victim to emotional manipulation; it has nothing to do with weakness.

14. **Myth:** After love bombing, you'll never be able to trust people again.
    Truth: With awareness and the right support, it's possible to rebuild trust in yourself and in future relationships.

15. **Myth:** Love bombing is always evident from the start.
    Truth: It can be hard to recognize immediately, as it presents itself as seemingly sincere gestures of affection.

Looking to the Future with Confidence

Now comes the most important phase: recognizing your worth and deciding never to settle for less than what you truly deserve. It's time to learn how to say "no" to anything that hurts you and "yes" to what helps you grow. Respect your emotional well-being and choose relationships that enrich you with sincere love.

Your past experiences don't define who you are, but they teach you valuable lessons about how to move forward with new eyes and make better choices. Each step toward greater awareness brings you closer to a life where love is real, free, and mutual.

You've already started this journey by reading this book. Now, continue with determination, knowing that you're stronger and more aware than ever. Choose the love you deserve: the one that builds, supports, and respects you. And never forget that you are the true guardian of your happiness and your heart. Every day is an opportunity to write a story that makes you proud to be who you are.

Open the Door to the New

As you close this chapter, new possibilities open up. Move forward with the knowledge that you deserve the best and that each step toward a happier, healthier life is an act of courage. Open yourself to new relationships, new beginnings, and love that truly reflects who you are.

www.ingramcontent.com/pod-product-compliance
Lightning Source LLC
LaVergne TN
LVHW021828060526
838201LV00058B/3556